FAITH AND FESTIVITY

To four worship 'critics' —
Jonathan, Timothy, Susannah and Benjamin

Faith
and
Festivity

A guide for today's worship leaders

PAUL BEASLEY-MURRAY

MARC
Eastbourne

Cover design by W. James Hammond

British Library Cataloguing in Publication Data

Beasley-Murray, Paul
    Faith and festivity
    1. Nonconformist churches. Public worship
    I. Title
    264

    ISBN 1–85424–136–2

Printed in Great Britain for
MARC, an imprint of Monarch Publications Ltd
1 St Anne's Road, Eastbourne, E Sussex BN21 3UN by
Richard Clay Ltd, Bungay, Suffolk.
Typeset by J&L Composition Ltd, Filey, North Yorkshire

CONTENTS

INTRODUCTION

Christian worship, declared Karl Barth, the greatest theologian of this century, is 'the most momentous, the most urgent, the most glorious action that can take place in human life'.[1] Worship is the occasion when men and women become truly alive, when we humans, made in the image of God, begin to fulfil the very purpose of our existence by relating to the God who made us. It is that moment when we are caught up into heaven itself and join with the multitude around the throne, singing the praises of God and the Lamb. In the words of the ancient *Sursum Corda*:

> Therefore with angels and archangels,
> and with all the company of heaven,
> we proclaim your great and glorious name,
> for ever praising you and saying:
> Holy, holy, holy Lord,
> God of power and might,
> heaven and earth are full of your glory.
> Hosanna in the highest!

Worship is the business of heaven. In worship we anticipate the day when, in the words of St Augustine, 'we shall do nothing other than ceaselessly repeat Amen and Alleluia, with insatiable satisfaction'. It is in worship that heaven invades our world, and we discover ourselves in the presence of Almighty God. What an experience! What a privilege!

No doubt all of us can look back on those occasions when God broke into our worship in a way never to be forgotten. I, for one, can think back to a whole host of occasions when heaven itself was open for me and when, with Isaiah of old, I saw the Lord on a throne, high and lifted up. A very traditional Baptist Union Assembly of Wales meeting, singing the praises of God in minor key; a Spring Harvest celebration, charismatic in flavour, with brass sounding and drums rolling; a quiet celebration of the Lord's Supper with only a dozen or so people in a remote Lake District chapel; an overflowing expectant congregation celebrating God's praise in the context of a baptismal service — on all these occasions and many more, God has broken in.

Anne Ortlund, wife of Ray Ortlund, one-time pastor of the Lake Avenue Congregational Church in Pasadena, California, captures something of the wonder of worship in the introduction to her book *Is Your Church Real?*

> I don't know about you. If you've never been in church when God was obviously present, may this book make you so thirsty for that to happen, you'll be absolutely cotton-mouthed. If you have — do you remember? Stop and recall. Oh holy, glorious, sweaty-palms time! If you were the leader, you wondered when — how — if you should put a lid on this bubbling pot! One thing is sure: you knew: Oh, God, this is what I was made for. This is stretching and rewarding and fulfilling, down deep in my bones. This is Eternity Business. I'm being caught up into the Important. This is — breaking into glory![2]

Yes, there is no experience which can compare to Christian worship. It is indeed, 'the most glorious action that can take place in human life'.

Crisis in worship

And yet, if the truth be told, for me — and I believe for many others too — there is a very real crisis taking place precisely in this area of worship. Far too often worship is dissatisfying, it is frustrating, it is downright disappointing. God does not break in, boredom breaks out. It doesn't matter whether I am in a festival crowd of several thousand or in an ordinary service with just fifty or so present, whether the congregation is charismatic or non-charismatic — worship for the most part is a let-down.

Realism demands that we should not expect to be swept off our feet by the Spirit of God on every occasion. We cannot live life forever on the mountain tops. Thus John Wesley spoke of certain religious feelings as 'sweet meats' to be enjoyed now and again, but not the staple diet of Christians.[3] But never have I felt so frustrated with worship as I do now. No doubt some will say that this in part must be due to the fact that I am no longer running my own 'show', I am no longer pastor of a local church, but rather an itinerant preacher who only spasmodically attends his local church. However, I believe that the fact that I am no longer pastor of one church, but rather in a whole succession of different churches most Sundays, gives me a wider perspective and clearer insight into the problem we face: a crisis of worship.

In my book *Dynamic Leadership* (p 145ff), I identified two related causes of this present crisis. First of all, in many circles worship has become man-centered; the emphasis is upon our feelings. We spend much of our time telling God how we feel, as an examination of any collection of modern songs quickly reveals. Furthermore, there is a tendency to expect that worship should always make us feel good. Instead of coming to worship God because he is God, we come to worship God because we need a boost. 'Join us for worship', declared a noticeboard outside a church, 'you will feel better for it'. But is that necessarily true? If God is to the fore, we may not initially feel better at all. An encounter with God may actually prove to be painful and may entail a call to sacrifice, commitment and self-denial. In the words of Ralph Martin: 'The call is not so much "Smile God loves you", as "Repent", "Weep", "Tremble"'.[4]

Secondly, much contemporary evangelical worship has lost its sense of direction. The sense of movement implicit in some of the traditional orders of service has been abandoned, and little of substance has been put in their place. Don't get me wrong. I have no doubt that the old 'hymn-sandwich', into which the traditional Reformed order of service degenerated, has had its day. I delight in the movement of charismatic renewal, which has swept through so many of our churches, bringing with it a fresh understanding of worship and a fresh desire to worship God. How much poorer contemporary worship would be without the new songs. God has indeed poured out his Spirit upon his people in a new way. But the 'new wine' of his Spirit is heady stuff. It has burst its old containers. It needs new wineskins, new worship structures, if it is to be contained. Alas, in many free and independent evangelical churches there are no structures. Worship for the most part lacks form, and therefore lacks direction. Many pastors have abdicated their traditional role of leading worship and handed it over to the church's musicians, without apparently realising that there is a great difference between leading songs and leading worship.

If worship is to be truly satisfying, if worship is to lead into the presence of God, if worship is to provide the norms and inspiration for living, then there must be structure and direction. Freedom without form all too often means that worship becomes a man-centered emotional experience, which does not actually meet the needs of the heart. In other words, even in non-liturgical churches, the worship leader needs to have a sense of liturgy. It is to this need that this particular book is directed — its purpose is to enable worship-leaders to have an understanding of the art and of the science that is theirs.

Worship and life

A further word of introduction needs to be said: worship must always be related to real life. This book is concerned with worship in the context of a church service. Worship, of course, must spill out beyond these narrow confines. There is no true worship which does not result in a life of obedience. As a result of having come together to worship God, we must not only see life in a new perspective — we must also go out and live life in the light of that new perspective. Worship must never be an experience isolated from the world. If worship fails to relate to life, then it fails to be genuine. The message of Amos 5:21, 23–24 needs to be taken seriously: 'I hate, I despise your religious feasts, I cannot stand your assemblies. . . . Away with the noise of your songs! I will not listen to the music of your harps. But let justice roll on like a river, righteousness like a never-failing stream!' It is not that God doesn't like us to sing songs of praise — but songs make him sick if they are an expression of mere religiosity. True worship must make a difference to the way we live our lives. Indeed, the life we live in the world can be as much worship as the praise we offer up in our church services (see Hebrews 13:15–16).

Faith and festivity

One final word of explanation is perhaps called for. This book is divided into two sections. The first section, entitled 'Celebrating the Faith' deals with the general principles of Christian worship. The second section, entitled 'Celebrating the Festivals', deals with the particular application of these principles to those Christian festivals many a church will celebrate during the year.

It may well be that this second section, with its emphasis on the observance of the Christian year, needs some explanation as far as some nonconformists are concerned. In some circles the observance of such specials days has been frowned on, and texts such as Galatians 4:10 and Colossians 2:16 have been cited in support of non-observance. One such nonconformist was my maternal grandfather, a devout Plymouth brother who, as a mark of protest against the observances of the Established Church, would always take the family down to the seaside on Good Friday.

While recognising the dangers of empty ritualism and also liturgical fundamentalism, I believe there is much to be said for observing the high days of the Christian year. Celebrating the Christian festivals adds richness and colour to worship. Whatever the predilections of the preacher, it ensures that in worship the congregation has a regular opportunity to focus upon the main events in our Lord's life. If the truth be told, some nonconformists have protested too much. A return to celebrating the festivals — as well as the faith — is surely well and truly right.

PART 1

CELEBRATING THE FAITH

I

Giving God the Glory
— the service begins

Giving God the glory

The English word 'worship' derives from the Saxon 'weorthscipe' which became 'worthship' or the acknowledgement of worship. Therefore to worship God means to acknowledge God's worth, to tell him how he actually is, to give him the glory.

Worship is a giving of ourselves and of our praises to God. Worship is an event in which every worshipper is actively involved. Søren Kierkegaard, the Danish philosopher and theologian of the last century, used to say that worship is a drama in which the congregation is the actor and God is the audience. Unfortunately, in our entertainment-orientated society there is a very real danger that the up-front personalities (the pastor, the worship leader, members of the music, dance or drama group) may appear to be the players rather than those whose task it is to lead the entire congregation to 'perform' (ie, worship). Hence we may hear such comments from the congregation as 'I really enjoyed the worship today', or 'I didn't get anything from the worship today', as if in worship we primarily receive rather than give. However, in the first place worship is for God, and God alone. Worship inevitably focuses on God. It is a turning away from self and a gazing upon God in such a manner that praise

15

and adoration, confession and penitence, dedication and commitment are our response. In true worship, God is at the centre.

At first sight there may appear to be nothing revolutionary in such statements, and yet they contrast vividly with so much man-centered worship. Thus it is not uncommon for a service of worship to begin with a hymn such as 'Who is on the Lord's side?', where the emphasis is on challenge rather than praise; for the following prayers to focus exclusively on ourselves — our feelings, our expectations, our needs, our sins, our response to God. The worship could then continue with further songs such as 'Rejoice! Rejoice! Christ is in you' or 'For this purpose Christ was revealed', where again the emphasis is on us, rather than on God! Needless to say, there is nothing wrong with such hymns and songs provided they are in their rightful place — as part of our response to all that God is and has done for us. Worship, however, must begin with God.

Christian worship, too, must focus on the Son of God — our Lord Jesus Christ. It is interesting that the vast majority of the hymns in the opening section of the *Baptist Hymn Book*, entitled 'Worship and Praise', do not even mention Jesus, let alone declare his praises. For the most part they focus on God as Creator. Clearly, we should praise God for the wonderful world which he has made, but if our praise is limited to his creative activity, then our praise is one-sided. In this respect it is helpful to listen to the prayers of children in church: God is consistently thanked as the one who has provided us with food to eat, clothes to wear, parents and teachers to care for us — but often that is as far as the prayer goes. Surely, the God and Father of our Lord Jesus Christ is supremely to be worshipped as the God who sent his Son to be our Saviour. Strangely, this truth is not always central to praise. Unitarians might feel very much at home in some Christian Churches.

Christian worship must focus on the God who raised Jesus

from the dead. The resurrection is the supreme act of God in Christ. As Paul made so clear in 1 Corinthians 15, the Christian faith stands or falls with the resurrection of Jesus: 'If Christ has not been raised, your faith is futile; you are still in your sins. ... But Christ has indeed been raised from the dead, the firstfruits of those who have fallen asleep ... 'Where O death, is your victory? Where, O death is your sting?' ... Thanks be to God! He gives us the victory through our Lord Jesus Christ' (1 Cor 15:17, 20, 55, 57). And yet, from careful observation, I know that it is possible for a visitor to attend many a nonconformist service and not to hear so much as a whisper about the resurrection, either in the hymns, or in the prayers, or in the sermon. How strange! How is it that the 'community of the resurrection', meeting as it does on the first day of the week, fails to celebrate God's triumph over sin and death, reserving its Easter praises to Easter day alone? True Christian worship will, every Sunday, express praise to God for Jesus, crucified and risen.

Celebrating the faith

If God has triumphed in the cross and resurrection, then this surely means that to give God the glory involves celebration. Let's not be afraid of this word 'celebration'; it reflects a very real aspect of worship. God is King! Jesus is Lord! 'Come, let us sing for joy to the Lord, let us shout aloud to the Rock of our salvation' (Ps 95:1) exclaimed the Psalmist. For him, joy was a key-note in worship. From our side of the cross and resurrection, there is even more reason to rejoice in God's kingly power and gracious love. Alas, Christians have not always known how to rejoice. There is a story about a pastor who once said to his congregation that if anyone watched them coming to church, that person would think they were on their way to the dentist, and if the same person watched them coming away from church, he would be sure they had been! Thank God such a criticism can no longer be made of most churches: the sober suits and faces to match are on the way out. Our worship is beginning to be less purely cerebral.

However, in some quarters there is still a resistance to the kind of worship that involves, as it were, giving 'three cheers' for God. Spring Harvest and other gatherings seem 'over the top'. Perhaps the attention of such critics needs to be drawn to the description of heaven's worship in Revelation 19:6–7 — 'Then I heard what sounded like a great multitude, like the roar of rushing waters and like loud peals of thunder, shouting: 'Hallelujah! For our Lord God Almighty reigns. Let us rejoice and be glad and give him glory!'. Whenever I read those verses I am reminded of Old Trafford or Cardiff Arms Park. The people who frequent those temples of sport know how to celebrate: banners fly, they wave their arms, they roar out the songs. Surely we too should learn to worship God 'with hearts and hands and voices'. Let's not be afraid of enthusiasm — it's better than the chill of the morgue any time!

On the other hand, celebration is more than having a happy time it is making God a 'celebrity'. Such celebration will be marked by joy, but at times it may also be characterised by deep reverence and awe. For the God we worship is awesome, both in his greatness and holiness: 'Come, let us bow down in worship, let us kneel before the Lord our Maker' (Ps 95:6) declared the same Psalmist, who encouraged us to 'shout aloud to the Rock of our salvation'. True, we can call God 'Abba' but that is no excuse for slapping him on the back and calling out 'Hi Dad!'. Reverence is our Father's due.

It is so easy to go to extremes. Some charismatics are full of froth and bubble, while some devotees of liturgical niceties are as correct as the corpse in an American funeral parlour! Let us encourage those we lead in worship to celebrate, but let us ensure that such celebration is also mixed with awe.

The service begins

How does all this work out in practice? How, in practical terms, can the congregation be led to give of themselves in worship to God? Let me give an example of an opening act of worship, and then comment on it:

(Preparation for worship)
Call to worship
Opening hymn/songs of worship
Prayer of praise and thanksgiving
Prayer of confession
The Lord's Prayer
Scripture
Songs of worship

Preparation for worship

Strictly speaking, preparation for worship is not part of an order of service — hence the brackets in the above order. And yet it belongs there. Ideally, the service begins before the clock chimes 11 am or whenever. It begins as people prepare themselves for worship between their arrival and the service's formal commencement. Hence, as a pastor, I used to say to my people: if you are are not five minutes early for service, then you are ten minutes late. For me — as surely for many others too — those few minutes of silent prayer can make all the difference as we focus on God. We warm ourselves up, as it were, so that we are ready for 'lift-off' when the worship leader says, 'Let us worship God.'

But is such talk of preparation for worship realistic in many churches today? The period before worship has become the time for welcoming one another and exchanging the latest news. The church is a place of tremendous hubbub. The worship leader stills the crowd with difficulty.

How can we ensure that there is time for preparation? In some churches it is customary to have a few minutes of singing songs of worship. The difficulty here is that if it is not actually part of the formal worship service, there will always be those who treat it as an optional extra and carry on talking to their friends. One London church has a cross at the front of the worship area, which lights up a few minutes before the start of the service. In the words of their weekly news sheet, this 'is to remind you that the pastor and deacons have commenced a short session of prayer, asking God's blessing on all that shall be said and done during the service. We ask the congregation also to observe a time of quietness in preparation for the service'. (Unfortunately, that practice reminds me of a crematorium, where the cross lit up as the curtains were drawn round the coffin!)

On the Continent many churches signal the time for personal preparation with an organ prelude. Up until that point there has been no 'musical wallpaper', as is our custom. But suddenly the organ breaks in and all fall silent. A custom which I have seen work in several churches is for a deacon to call the congregation to worship — or should I say to 'order' — by reading a few verses from a Psalm or some other appropriate scripture. This is then followed by a few moments of silence before the service formally begins. Even children can be encouraged to be still for just a few minutes.

Call to worship

If preparation for worship has in fact taken place, then such a 'call to worship' is, strictly speaking, a call to continue to worship. With a verse or two of Scripture, the worship leader helps the congregation to focus on the love and grace of God, or whatever the attribute the following hymn or song focuses on.

A hymn of praise/songs of worship

'If anybody is happy, let him sing songs of praise' writes James (Jas 5:13). The songs that we sing at the beginning of our worship are to be songs of praise in which God's worth, rather than our feelings, is declared. Ralph Martin helpfully talks of such worship in the following manner:

The life of praise is the hallmark of Christian existence, since it demonstrates that the believing community has already anticipated the last day of God's final victory and is stretching out to share in its glories, even if the end is not yet attained. ... Praise acts as the litmus test to decide whether or not men are on God's side.

Our opening worship should make very clear whose side we are on.[5]

I confess that I am a great believer in opening the worship with a traditional hymn rather than a modern song. Well-known hymns are more likely to unite the congregation in praise than songs which may be known to some, but perhaps not to all. Clearly, however, congregations vary considerably and so generalisations are well-nigh impossible.

Whether it be with a hymn or a modern worship song, it is important to give the congregation time to 'warm up'. The hymn needs to be fairly long, or alternatively, several worship songs could be chosen. For in spite of the period of preparation, not everybody is ready to worship God with their whole being. The hymn or the songs need to be aids to worship, rather than simply vehicles of worship — they help to get people into the mood to worship. F.H. Brabant makes the point in this way:

If we all arrived (at church) feeling and thinking as we ought, no doubt our services would be simply the expression in speech and action of the inner state of our souls with all the spontaneous directness of children. But we do not, most of us, arrive like that. We come, stained and weary from a life that is largely unnatural, longing for something to lift us up into an atmosphere of peace.[6]

Hence worship 'has not only an expressive function, but also a suggestive or impressive one'. John Wesley said the same thing in a different way when commending his original collection of hymns, which he dedicated to every pious reader, as a means of raising or quickening the spirit of devotion or confirming his faith, enlivening his hope, and of kindling and increasing his love to God and men.

Because of this all-too necessary 'warming up' period, I confess that I am unhappy with the structure of many morning worship services, where by and large there is only one opportunity to 'give God the glory' — in the opening hymn or song. But many people are just not ready to do that so early on. By the time they are ready, it is time for the children's talk!

Prayers of praise and thanksgiving

The theme of praise is taken up in the opening prayer of praise and thanksgiving. The prayer should link naturally with the preceding hymn so that there is a natural 'flow' to the praise. As we have already said, our praise for God's goodness should centre on Jesus. Hebrews 12:2 should be the motto: 'Let us fix our eyes on Jesus.'

There is much to be said for the opening prayer being credal in character. Noncomformists may not recite the creed, but this is no reason why they should not declare their faith in their prayers (as, of course, in their hymns). Those who lead in prayer should enable the congregation every Sunday to praise God for Christ crucified, risen, ascending, reigning, returning. . . . Here is the 'raw meat' of the Gospel. How anaemic so much prayer is today, centering on peripherals rather than on the heart of the Christian faith.

Prayer of confession

In many churches today this prayer is omitted. Yet, Sunday by Sunday, we all need an opportunity to confess our sins and begin afresh with God. The sooner that happens in the service the better.

Confession naturally issues from praise, for it is as we focus on God and discover afresh who he is that we are reminded again of our unworthiness. Our God is a holy God, whose 'eyes are too pure to look on evil' and who 'cannot tolerate wrong' (Hab 1:13). Sometimes we forget this aspect of God. Jamie Wallace, highlights this aspect of worship when he writes:

In worship, whether we lead or are led, but especially if we lead, we must realise the ineffable privilege of being able to worship God *with impunity*. If an ancient Hebrew rode the time machine to the front door of a Baptist church one Sunday morning, saw us going in, and understood what we were doing (ie, from his point of view entering the Holy of Holies without being high priests) he would not expect us to come out alive![7]

Our God is also a merciful God. Again, the congregation need to be reminded of this. In the Anglican and Roman Catholic churches the priest declares God's pardon as he pronounces absolution. In nonconformist churches, pastors do not have such a priestly role. However, there is no reason why we should not allow the Scriptures to speak the word of absolution. Indeed, there is every good reason to give the congregation the opportunity to hear such 'comfortable' words as 'the blood of Jesus his Son purifies us from all sin . . . If we confess our sins, he is faithful and just and will forgive us our sins and purify us from all unrighteousness' (1 Jn 1:7, 9).

The Lord's Prayer

'This is how you should pray: "Our Father in heaven, hallowed be your name." (Mt 6:9–13; Lk 11:2–4). This is more than a model prayer, it is a prayer intended to be prayed. This can be deduced from the 'striking fact that when the prayer taught by Jesus is put back into his own language, both in Matthew's version and in Luke's version, it has rhythm and rhyme. Jewish poetry did not rhyme, apart from a notable exception — the prayer said by Jews three times daily (the Eighteen Benedictions)'[8]

In the light of this fact it seems good to ensure that the congregation has an opportunity to pray the Lord's Prayer at least once a Sunday. In so far as it begins and ends with praise, it can fit very well toward the beginning of the service; on the other hand, it can fit almost anywhere else too. One thing is for sure, whenever this prayer is prayed within the context of contemporary worship, it makes sense for the congregation to pray it in contemporary language. In this regard, the version produced by the Joint Liturgical Group is to be commended:

Our Father in heaven,
hallowed be your name,
your kingdom come,
your will be done,
on earth as in heaven.
Give us today our daily bread.
Forgive us our sins
as we forgive those who sin against us.
Lead us not into temptation
but deliver us from evil.
For the kingdom, the power and glory are yours
now and for ever. Amen

The congregation will probably need to make an effort to adjust to the modern wording, but once the adjustment is made it will realise how strange it was to pray the Lord's Prayer in language belonging to past centuries rather than today.

Scripture

Scripture included at this stage in the service should inspire us to deeper praise. These scriptures are not the 'lessons' for the day, which will form the preacher's text, but rather, in the words of Eleanor Kreider serve as 'the sticks and logs for the worship fire'.[9] In the light of God's revelation of himself in his word, the congregation responds again in praise.

Songs of praise

Thank God for modern worship songs! They make a delightful balance to some of the older hymns. There is no one kind of church hymnody — variety is needed. Calvin got it wrong when he said, 'The music of hymns should not be light and sprightly; it should have weight and majesty, and thus there should be a marked difference between the music which is played to delight men at table and in their homes, and that of the psalms sung in church and in the presence of his angels.'[10] Provided music can be a vehicle for worship, then it is valid within worship.

On the other hand, we need to recognise that songs, like hymns, can vary enormously in quality. The worship leader needs to take care in choosing which songs to sing. Eleanor Kreider somewhat amusingly comments: 'Some new songs get worn out very quickly. They're like paper towels — they're suitable for one job, but they disintegrate with use.'[11]

Again, we need to take care in the number of times we repeat a song. In some churches it is almost an unwritten law that a song is sung at least twice. However, there is no reason why this should always be so — just as there is no reason why some of the songs should not be repeated. In this regard, John Leach makes an interesting contrast between the use of modern worship songs and formal liturgies:

> They [the songs] are designed to be known and learned by heart, they are repetitive, and they are used to their greatest effect when they have gone so deep into one's being that they flow spontaneously out again in worship. This is exactly the way liturgy should be used, and 'non-liturgical' churches have a lot to teach about how to do it.[12]

2

Praying Together
— and for others

Praying together

Praying in public

There is a very real difference between public and private prayer. Public prayer is not simply private prayer amplified through a microphone with others listening in. Public prayer involves the worship leader bringing the congregation together before the throne of grace. Those who lead in public prayer therefore need to adopt a different style from the one they may use in their private devotions.

This public style is particularly marked by the use of the first person plural rather than the first person singular. Instead of saying, 'I thank you Lord,' the leader now says, 'We thank you Lord.' The leader becomes the mouthpiece of the community, vocalising their prayers and not just his or her's. Inevitably this means that public prayer is less personal than private prayer. Prayers of confession, for instance, become more general as it is no longer possible to be so specific. Everybody in the congregation needs to be able to identify with public prayers.

Public prayer must also be immediately intelligible. There is no place for the rarified prayer, full of scriptural allusions, which only the initiated can understand. Latinisms and archaisms should be avoided. So too should unnecessary theological jargon. The language of the ordinary person in the pew should be the order of the day. The style adopted by the *Good News Bible* is much to be commended. The task of the worship leader is not to impress the congregation with fine phrases and felicitous expressions of speech, but rather to enable fellow worshippers to draw near to God. 'In the presence of the Lord of hosts,' said Spurgeon, 'it ill becomes the sinner to parade the feathers and finery of tawdry speech with the view of winning applause from his fellow mortals.'[13]

From this it follows that prayer must always be addressed to God. The prayer of one American pastor was said to be 'the most eloquent ever offered to a Boston congregation'! Prayer should not seek to impress — nor, for that matter, should it try to admonish or to impart information. Some pastors address their congregation through the medium of prayer. But for prayer to be prayer, it must be addressed to God — and not horizontally to the congregation.

Prayer is multifaceted

Prayer has been likened to a white ray of sunlight, broken by a prism into the colours of the spectrum. In other words, there are many different types of prayer, all of which have their place in a service of worship.

1) *Prayer of invitation.* This is sometimes called the prayer of 'invocation' (from the Latin for 'to call upon') in which we call upon God to assist us in the worship we offer. Traditionally, there are three places in a service of worship where this might take place: in the opening prayer; in the prayer before the sermon (the prayer for 'illumination'); as part of the eucharistic prayer (sometimes called '*epiclesis*', which comes from a Greek verb meaning 'to call upon'). It is this prayer of invitation which lies at the root of the custom in charismatic circles today of inviting the Holy Spirit to be present in the worship.

2) *Prayer of adoration or praise.* In this prayer God's worth is extolled. This is the heart of worship. 'The language of

adoration pays homage to the surpassing majesty of God and sings his amazing love for his creatures and his unexampled grace for sinners.'[14] Our needs and the needs of others are totally forgotten. God and God alone is the focus of attention. It has been said that 'without adoration, there will be nothing to lift our services above the level of human hopes and dreams. Adoration provides the wings that lift us from self to God; it is the divine wind which fills our sails and sends us across the sea to God from the tiny little harbour of our own lives'.[15] Such praise or adoration rightly belongs to the beginning of the service — but it will also find expression elsewhere. It comes to particular focus as believers celebrate the Lord's Supper.

3) *Thanksgiving*. This is closely linked to adoration. Sometimes thanksgiving is distinguished from adoration on the ground that in adoration we centre our thoughts on God and on what he is in himself (his holiness, splendour, beauty and majesty), whereas in thanksgiving we remember what God is and does in relation to us. However, the distinction is not so clearcut. We cannot, for instance, easily focus on God and his love without immediately becoming conscious of what God has done for us in Christ. So much of what we know of God is inevitably linked with ourselves. However, though the distinction between adoration and thanksgiving is not always clear, there is surely a difference of emphasis: in adoration the emotion is primarily that of awe, in thanksgiving it is primarily that of gratitude. There is so much, of course, for which we can be grateful. Christian thanksgiving, however, will focus in particular on Jesus, God's greatest gift. In the words of the General Thanksgiving: 'We bless you for our creation, preservation, and all the blessings of this life; but above all for your immeasurable love in the redemption of the world by our Lord Jesus Christ, for the means of grace, and for the hope of glory.'

4) *Prayer of confession*. It is as we focus on God and on what he has done for us in Jesus that we become conscious of

our own unworthiness and sinfulness. Adoration and thanksgiving inevitably lead to penitence. In the words of the prophet Isaiah: 'I saw the Lord seated on a throne, high and exalted. ... "Woe to me!" I cried. "I am ruined! For I am a man of unclean lips, and I live among a people of unclean lips, and my eyes have seen the king, the Lord Almighty" (Is 6:1, 5). In Isaiah's vision 'confession' was also followed by 'absolution': a seraph touched Isaiah's mouth with one of the live coals and said, 'your guilt is taken away and your sin atoned.' Likewise in Christian worship the congregation is (traditionally) assured of their forgiveness in Christ.

5) *Prayer of intercession.* Here we bring the needs of others before God. Geoffrey Wainwright defines this prayer as 'a plea for the triumph of the divine purpose in spite of contrary expectations'.[16] Here we seek God's best for his world.

6) *Prayer of petition.* Sometimes called 'supplication', this is when we bring our own needs to God. In public worship this normally means asking for particular graces to help the congregation to be the kind of people God wants them to be. More specific petition is only possible where the worship leader gives space for silent prayer, in which individual worshippers bring their particular needs before God. In this way we fulfil Peter's injunction: 'Cast all your anxiety on him because he cares for you' (1 Pet 5:7).

7) *Prayer of dedication.* This is sometimes called the prayer of 'oblation' (from the Latin *'oblatio'*, meaning offering), in which we rededicate ourselves to the service of God. This may find expression at various points in the service: in the prayer following the offering, in which not only gifts but givers are presented to the Lord; in the prayer following the sermon (the prayer of 'response'); as we celebrate the Lord's Supper and respond afresh to God's love.

In any given service all seven prayers should find their place. The words of R.E.O. White need to be heeded:

The pastor may sometimes suspect that for some of his fellow-worshippers, the prayer-time in church is the only period of the week deliberately set apart for praying. He will want to make the very most of it for their sake. So by example he will strive to show that without thanksgiving prayer is not worthy to be offered; without adoration it is not truly prayer to God; without confession it is not honest, and without petition it is not prayer at all; without intercession it is not Christian — and without sincere, believing prayer even public worship in the house of God is a profitless pretence.[17]

Should prayer be free?

In contrast with the set prayers of the Anglican and Roman Catholic Churches, the Free Church has traditionally had free forms of prayer. Not for them the Prayer Book! Ever since the Great Ejection of 1661, Free Churchmen have been proud of their freedom to address God in whatever manner they deem fit.

Today, however, things are beginning to change. Free prayer can be found in some Anglican and Roman Catholic churches, and in some Free churches set prayers can be heard. What are the advantages and disadvantages of both these forms of prayer?

Set forms of prayer

1) *Advantages*

- They save the congregation from being at the mercy of the worship leader's moods, which may well vary according to weather, health or general feelings.
- They are normally carefully constructed, and therefore often have an intrinsic beauty and dignity.
- Set prayers often have an element of catholicity about them. Worshippers are linked with others up and down the land using the same prayer book; and where the prayers are centuries old, worshippers are linked with the church of the past.

2) *Disadvantages*

- There is no room for the spontaneous inspiration of the Spirit. The Spirit's inspiration is limited to the past.
- Set prayers inevitably lack particularity. No set prayer can ever be perfectly suited to every occasion — there is always a certain generality of expression.
- Unless carefully (prayerfully) read, set prayers tend towards unreality, particularly when taken from a prayer book being used by the congregation.

Free prayer

The advantages and disadvantages of free prayer for the most part are a mirror image of the advantages and disadvantages of set prayer.

1) *Advantages*

- Free prayers have a greater feel of spontaneity about them. The very form expresses something of the believer's relationship with his God. As Stephen Winward put it: 'Warm, direct, intimate, personal extempore prayer corresponds to the nature of prayer as conversation with God'.[18]
- Free prayer is very relevant to the needs of the congregation and of the wider world. By its very nature free prayer can be both immediate and particular.
- Free prayer has a greater feeling of reality about it. It is more immediately perceived as a conversation with God. The focus is God — not initially the printed page!

2) *Disadvantages*

- As mentioned above, the congregation can be at the mercy of the worship leader's moods, which in turn can result in a lack of objectivity.
- Where free prayer is the order of the day, the language of the one who leads in prayer can become stereotyped, repeating well-worn phrases and pious cliches.

• In the past, at least, free prayer could be wordy and meandering, long and tedious. A Congregationalist of a past era, Bernard Manning, once wrote: 'I still feel something of the horror with which the Long Prayer always affected me when I was a boy. Everywhere it was the same. There appeared to be no chance it would ever end. You simply resigned yourself. Time after time occurred places at which an admirable ending could have been made; but no, 'Pray without ceasing': that apostolic word had been only too carefully observed. I watched the sunbeam broken in windows and caught in the gilt of the hymn book covers; I played every kind of game and then, at last, it was over: and we raised our heads, it seemed to me, like people coming out of our huts after a tornado anxious to see who is still there and who is missing'.

The contrast, however, is not just between 'set' prayer and 'free' prayer, for there are two forms of free prayer. Isaac Watts, distinguished between '*conceived*' or prepared free prayer 'done by some work of meditation before we begin to speak in prayer' and *extempore* free prayer 'when we without any reflection or meditation beforehand address ourselves to God and speak the thoughts of our hearts as fast as we conceive them'.[19]

While extempore free prayer may be the order of the day in the home and in prayer meetings, there is much to be said for the prepared free prayer in public services of worship — especially if one is leading the same congregation in worship Sunday by Sunday. The extent of such preparation may well vary. Sometimes the preparation will just be making headings, sometimes it may take the form of fairly full notes, and sometimes a prayer may even be written out in full. I would encourage pastors to consider adopting the discipline of writing out one prayer a week. This would encourage a better use of language, including simplicity and variety of expression. There are two advantages to prepared free prayer: on the one hand, it ensures room for complete freedom and spontaneity; on the other, it ensures that the content is balanced and ordered.

Beware of pitfalls

Those who pray extempore need to be aware of a number of pitfalls:

1) *Mind your language*! Exponents of free prayer need to take care of the words they use. Most difficulties would be overcome if those who prayed, prayed naturally: ie, if they prayed to God as though they were actually addressing their own father. I have in mind not just the two extremes of pomposity and slang, but also evangelical jargon which can detract from prayer. For instance, the little word 'just' appears far too often in prayer, as does 'share' and 'minister' ('Father, we *just* want to *share* with you our concern for those who are *ministering* today'). Sickening sentimentalism ('Sweet Lord', 'Precious Lord') may have suited the Victorians, but it doesn't suit people today. The language of Zion ('Lord, we bless you that we have washed our robes in the blood') is foreign to most ears — although it is true that the judicious use of Scripture within prayer can be helpful. Fortunately the era of addressing God in seventeenth-century language is past, but some people still mix in the occasional 'Thee' and 'Thou', especially when quoting from Scripture. To be natural is to be direct: there is no need to pray, 'Lord we *would* ask you,' or 'We pray that you *might* act.' Far better, 'Father, please help.' To be natural is also to be simple: instead of thanking God for being 'justified' in Christ, thank him for being 'put right'. Unneccesary technical terms should be avoided. We should use the kind of language that a twelve-year-old would understand. Remember, too, that words derived from Anglo-Saxon as distinct from Latin and French are normally stronger and thus more effective. Closely associated with the language used in prayer is the

language used to introduce prayer: to ask the question 'Shall we pray?' is to invite the possibility of someone answering 'No!'. Far better to give a strong lead, using such words as, 'Let us pray,' or, 'We shall now pray.'

2) *Mind the length*. Jesus himself told his disciples that nothing is gained by praying at length: 'And when you pray, do not keep on babbling like pagans, for they think they will be heard for their many words'. (Mt 6:7). Many a present-day worship leader needs to remember this. Children certainly cannot concentrate for any length of time, so when they are present, prayers need to be kept short and sweet. A two or three-minute opening prayer at the beginning of family worship is more than sufficient. But adults, too, are not able to concentrate for any length of time. The traditional 'long prayer' in many churches is therefore unhelpful. Far better to break it into a series of short prayers.

3) *Mind your subject*. To whom is prayer addressed? Although not writing specifically about prayer, Paul enunciates the principle when he says, 'Through him [Jesus] we both have access to the Father by one Spirit' (Eph 2:18). In other words, prayer is normally addressed to the Father by the Spirit, either through Jesus (Rom 1:8; 2 Cor 1:20) or in the name of Jesus (Mt 18:19, 20; Jn 16:23–24). This was certainly true of the New Testament church where for the most part prayer was not addressed to Jesus. C.F.D. Moule writes: 'Address direct to Christ is rare in the New Testament [his examples include Acts 7:59; 22:10, 1 Corinthians 16:22; 2 Corinthians 12:8], but address to God *through* Christ and benediction of God *for* his mighty deeds in Christ were normal.'[20] What is inexcusable is where the persons of the Trinity are confused: eg, 'Father, we do thank you for dying on the cross'!

Open prayer

As I have written this book for worship leaders, I have emphasised prayer led from the 'front'. In many churches today, however, there are opportunities for worshippers to participate in open prayer: in a time of 'open worship' where the emphasis is on praise; as part of the prayers of intercession; in response to what God has been saying through the sermon; or gathered around the Lord's Table responding to his grace. Open prayer therefore can be very varied. It is important that where opportunities are given for open prayer, such prayers should on the one hand be aubible to all (I know one church where in times of open prayer stewards walk up and down the aisles with roving microphones), and on the other hand be short and clearly focused.

Silent prayer

Not all prayer needs to be voiced. The worship leader can encourage silent prayer. As with open prayer, silent prayer can be varied. At the beginning of a service, the worship leader might exhort the congregation to be still and acknowledge the presence of God — in Quaker terminology, the congregation would then 'centre down' on God. Silent prayer can also be part of intercessory prayer, when it is preceded by a 'bidding': eg, 'Let us pray for X or Y,' or 'Let us pray for ourselves and the week that lies ahead.' In many churches silent prayer is customary as the congregation eats bread and drinks wine at the Lord's Table. Such times of silent prayer can be so helpful.

However, we need to heed the words of Stephen Winward: 'Silent prayer is demanding. To use it profitably requires concentration, discipline and dedication. It should therefore be used sparingly in a congregation in which there are differences of age and education, of experience and spirituality.'[21]

Prayer and the worship leader

Ultimately the key to public prayer lies not in public praying but in the worship leader's own private prayer life. The worship leader can only lead others to the throne of grace in so far as he himself has been there before. Charles Spurgeon states this truth eloquently: 'Habitual communion with God must be maintained, or our public prayers will be vapid or formal. If there be no melting of the glacier higher up in the ravines of the mountain, there will be no descending rivulets to cheer up the plain. Private prayer is the drill ground for our more public exercises.'[22]

Praying for others

A test of love

To pray for others is to show love towards others. This, surely, is the implication of the words of Jesus in Matthew 5:44 — '*Love* your enemies ... and *pray* for those who persecute you.' Dick France comments: 'Love ... is not just a sentimental feeling, but an earnest desire for their good.'[23] The intensity of our praying reveals the intensity of our loving.

If the truth be told, our love for others is very weak. It would be interesting, and probably highly disturbing, were we able to analyse the content of our own prayers. How seriously do we take the needs of others in our private devotions? R.E.O. White, gives some helpful advice: 'Private prayer can be an intensely self-absorbed and narrow-hearted exercise: the pastor's best antidote is not to lecture on how to pray, but a weekly exercise in intercession, informed and wide-ranging, for each other and the world.'[24]

The pastors of many non-liturgical churches no longer take the prayers of intercession seriously. Indeed, such prayers are simply not there. And there are such prayers which are, for the most part, limited to the immediate needs of the fellowship. The wider world is forgotten. It is not loved.

A test of obedience

The Scriptures make it clear that we are to pray for the world and its needs. Paul's words to Timothy come particularly to mind: 'I urge, then, first of all, that requests, prayers and intercession be made for everyone — for kings and all those in authority, that we may live peaceful and quiet lives in all godliness and holiness' (1 Tim 2:1–2). The breadth of intercessory prayer should have no bounds — 'everyone' is to be lifted before the throne of grace. Paul in verse 4, goes on to state that 'God wants all men to be saved and to come to a knowledge of the truth'. There is no limit to the love of God — neither should there be a limit to ours. Dick Williams, in his introduction to his collection of prayers entitled *Prayers for Today's Church*, writes: 'The range of every congregation's intercession must be as wide as the mass media's coverage. Indeed, it should be wider.' His prayers reflect that width — for there are prayers for entertainers, drop-outs, novelists, composers, psychiatrists, even for space travel. How his prayers contrast with the prayers heard in many a Baptist church!

It is important to recognise that Paul was not alone in encouraging the ministry of intercession. Thus Michael Vasey points out that our Lord, too, taught us to pray for the world:

> It is probably legitimate to see the petitions of the Lord's Prayer summarised in the plea, 'Your kingdom come.' This is much more than a request that God will help the church to grow and be good or that he will shore up the structures and institutions of society. It is a prayer for divine intervention that will bring radical, even traumatic, transformation. It will involve explicit acknowledgement of God ('hallowed be your name'), the meeting of human need ('daily bread'), reconciliation ('forgive as we forgive'), and mercy and deliverance in human anguish ('lead us not ... deliver ...').[25]

Vasey goes on to argue that, unlike 1 Timothy 2:2, 'to pray "your kingdom come" is to pray for change, to pray against as well as for the institutions of human society. To pray for judgment as well as peace'. When were you last in church, when judgement was invoked?

Patterns of intercession

If intercessory prayer is to have both breadth and balance, then a structure is helpful. The Anglican booklet *Intercessions for Use with Series 1 & 2 or Series 3 Holy Communion Services*, has the following structure:

- the church
- the world
- the local community
- the troubled
- the departed

Nonconformists may not want to pray for the departed, but the principle of dividing up intercessions in this way is helpful. At the very least the following three areas of concern should feature in the regular praying of the church:

- the church (local or overseas)
- the nation (or local community)
- the world

The task of the worship-leader is not just to reflect the concerns of the congregation. Rather those concerns must be extended. Needless to say, if the concerns of the church are to be extended, then those leading prayer must in the first place have broader concerns themselves. Such breadth can be gained by the use of missionary prayer calendars, which are inevitably wide-ranging; by reading through collections of prayers, which normally touch on all kinds of topics; by paying attention to the news, both at national and local level, and then using the headlines as items for prayer.

The ministry of intercession is an important and serious task, and deserves careful preparation. Sloppy, unprepared prayers reflect no real love for the world.

Short prayers

In nonconformist churches, the main prayer of intercession has traditionally been the 'long prayer'. I believe that a series of short prayers is much more helpful than one long prayer. Short prayers aid concentration, whereas long prayers run the danger of woolliness. D.L. Moody made an apt comment on this last point: 'Some people's prayers need to be cut off at both ends and set fire to in the middle.'

Short prayers are more directional and thus more clearly focused on particular people and areas of need. In this context, the advice of Michael Baughen is helpful: 'Pray for *people*, not institutions. God changes society by influencing people. So pray for Mrs Thatcher (even if you disagree with her!) rather than for right decisions at the EEC Summit.'[26] Prayers should always have 'bite', and never be just 'general'. To quote Michael Baughen again: 'Rather than pray for "all nurses", specify "Jill, one of our members, just starting as Sister of a ward on night duty."'. For prayers to be specific, the congregation needs to be informed. There is nothing worse, however, than giving out information in the prayer itself, thereby 'informing the Lord', as if he was unaware of a particular item of news or need!. Far better to share 'prayer concerns' before the actual time of prayer.

Short prayers enable people to participate more fully, in the sense that each prayer can be owned by saying a clear 'Amen'. The 'Amen' at the end of a 'long prayer', however, can have a different meaning. Thus Michael Taylor writes: 'The people's "Amen" should not degenerate into the minister's way of saying: "I've finished" (and, even worse, the congregation saying: "Thank God, he's finished"!).'[27]

The involvement of others

Needless to say, congregational involvement need not — and should not — be limited to saying 'Amen' to the prayers. Leading prayer should not be a ministerial monopoly, but a task shared with others. On the other hand, we need to take care that such sharing does not devalue the praying. Thus Charles Spurgeon who believed that the prayers of intercession were more important than the sermon, wrote: 'There must be no putting up of anybodies and nobodies to pray, and then the selection of the abler man to preach.'[28]

A variety of people may lead in prayer:

- The deacons and/or elders, as the spiritual leaders of the church, are 'naturals' to be invited to lead prayer.
- A 'ministry' team can be set up to concentrate on the specific ministry of leading intercessions. Members of such a team would meet together during the week to talk through, and pray about, the kind of concerns which should be brought to the church for prayer.
- From time to time, home groups could be invited to lead the prayers.
- Those members of the church who are at the 'sharp' end of life (eg, teachers, policemen, social workers) might be asked to share the concerns of their week, and then be invited to lead in prayer — better still, and then to be prayed for.
- The whole church could be involved in the intercessions. This involvement could take a variety of forms. The congregation could be invited to state their concerns, which the worship-leader would then write up on an overhead (precisely because the congregation's concerns can sometimes be narrow in extent, I believe it is helpful for the worship-leader to have done some preparation beforehand, and be ready with some additional suggestions of his own). These concerns do not then have to be itemised before the Lord one by one — the very act of writing them up can be viewed as an act of prayer. Alternatively, the congregation can be invited to participate in a time of open prayer. Where this is done, it is important that people are not only given guidance on what might be prayed for (I often spend a few minutes talking about three or four prayer concerns, and then invite three or four people to lead in prayer), but also be reminded that prayers should be clearly audible and focused on only one matter.

Guidelines for Intercessions

Precisely because leading intercessory prayer is such a responsible task, clear guidance must be given to those entrusted with it. In this respect Administry, *Let us pray*, have produced some excellent 'Guidelines for Leading Intercessions'.

Planning

- Keep prayers short and easy to concentrate on.
- Don't pray 'spur of the moment' prayers unless you are experienced and sure it is appropriate. They tend to ramble and waffle.
- An opening sentence/promise from the Bible can set the right tone or theme.
- Time yourself in advance, reading at 'prayer-speed'. Maximum time = . . . (minutes).

Writing prayers

- Have a short introduction to each prayer (never more than two sentences), telling people what it is about.
- Do not preach at people ('We pray that we may all give generously at the Gift Day'), or one-sidedly ('We pray that Labour will win').
- Use natural, modern language. Don't use phrases you would never use in conversation (eg, 'loved ones', 'afflicted').
- Include thanks to prevent it becoming a shopping list.
- Mention people in need by name, but check that they have given their consent. Cover yourself against the charge of leaving someone out by adding 'and others whom we name silently ourselves'.
- It is often good to leave silences for people to add their own requests, provided you explain what you are doing. Leave at least thirty seconds up to one minute.
- Make sure people know how and when to end the prayer. If 'Amen', lead up to it with 'in Jesus' name', leave a slight pause, and then firmly say, 'Amen.'

At first sight these guidelines may seem over-simplistic. Experience will soon prove how helpful they can be.

One final word of advice

Let me round off this chapter on prayer with some advice from C.H. Spurgeon:

> It is my solemn conviction that the prayer is one of the most weighty, useful, and honourable parts of the service, and that it ought to be even more considered than the sermon. ... Let your prayers be earnest, full of fire, vehemence, prevalence. ... Let your petitions be plain and heartfelt; and while your people may sometimes feel that the sermon was below the mark, may they also feel that the prayer compensated for all.[29]

3

Taking Scripture Seriously
— a balanced diet

Scripture in the life of the early church

The Apostle Paul wrote to Timothy urging him to 'Devote
yourself to the public reading of Scripture' (1 Tim 4:13).
Scripture in that context, of course, was not Scripture as we
know it — it was what Christians have come to call the Old
Testament. If the synagogue pattern of reading the Scriptures
was followed, then the readings would have included passages
from both the Law and the Prophets.

However, in addition to the Old Testament, letters from
Christian leaders were also read in the context of public
worship. Certainly this was true of Paul's letters: 'I charge
you before the Lord to have this letter read to all the
brothers' (1 Thess 5:26); 'After this letter has been read to
you, see that it is also read in the church of Laodicea and that
you in turn read the letter from Laodicea' (Col 4:16). Even
Paul's Letter to Philemon, though addressed to an individual,
was not intended to be private and confidential to Philemon,
but had the church in view, as the opening greeting indicates:
'To Philemon our dear friend and fellow-worker, to Apphia
our sister, to Archippus our fellow-soldier and to the church
that meets in your home' (Phil 1b,2).

The 'Epistles', although at that stage not recognised as
canonical Scripture, were part of the church's diet. What was
true of the Letters was also true of the Book of Revelation.

This 'tract for the times' was intended to be read in the churches of Asia Minor: 'Blessed is the one who reads the words of this prophecy, and blessed are those who hear it and take to heart what is written in it, because the time is near' (Rev 1:3; see also 22:16).

The Gospels would have formed part of public worship at an early stage in the church's development. For although the Gospels did not begin to be written down until thirty years after Christ's death, the 'traditions' enshrined in the Gospels almost certainly received verbal expression within church services. 'For I received from the Lord what I also passed on to you' (1 Cor 11:23–26) wrote Paul to the church at Corinth, as he reminded them of the institution of the Last Supper. It is widely believed that the narratives of the Passion came together in the eucharistic celebration of the early church. Similarly, it was in the context of worship that many of the words of Jesus would have been handed down.

Right from the beginning of the church's life, Scripture, both Old and New, had an important place.

Scripture in today's church

Would that it could also be said that Scripture in today's church still has an important place. Alas, this is not always the case. Indeed, strange to say, the more 'Bible-believing' a church might claim to be, the less Scripture may have a place.

In the more liturgical churches, Scripture still continues to play an important role within worship. Indeed, there are those in the Anglican church who would apparently argue that there is too much Scripture (see, for instance, T.G.A. Baker, *Questioning Worship* [SCM Press, 1977], pages 20–33). Thus in the liturgy of the Anglican Communion there are normally three readings — from the Old Testament, the Epistles, and the Gospels. This does not include any Psalms that may be sung, nor the Ten Commandments that might be read. Nor is one spared Scripture by attending straightforward Matins or Evensong — along with Old and New Testament readings, there are always one or two Psalms together with other passages of Scripture (eg, the Magnificat or the Nunc Dimittis) which find their way into the service. It is no exaggeration to say that the liturgy is literally peppered with Scripture.

Traditionally the Free Churches have also taken Scripture seriously. Thus the Congregationalist Raymond Abba, writing in the late 1950s, was able to say:

> In a full diet of worship all three Scripture lessons are necessary for an adequate setting forth of the Biblical revelation in the Christian perspective. The Old Testament reading, which should generally (although not necessarily) be taken from one of the prophetic books, tells of the preparation for the coming of Christ in the life and history of Israel; the Epistle testifies to the fellowship 'in Christ' of the New Israel; while in the Gospel the words and deeds of our Lord himself are set forth. ... The Lessons should be read in this order, the Gospel having the place of honour at the end as the seal of the Scriptures.[30]

Interestingly, Abba assumed that a Psalm would also be sung during the service of worship.

How different worship is in many a Free or independent church today. Where the constraints of a liturgical framework have been set aside, experience often shows that Scripture is downgraded. True, such churches would vigorously dispute that Scripture has been downgraded, for in theory they would have the highest regard for Scripture. Their practice, however, denies all their fine-sounding words regarding the inspiration and authority of Scripture: for by and large in many non-liturgical evangelical churches there is only one Scripture reading, and normally short at that. If there is a second Scripture reading, then it is often from the Psalms. As R.E.O. White acutely observes: 'Where the public reading of the Scripture is shortened to a minimum, the implied devaluation of the written word communicates itself to our people.'[31]

It is no exaggeration to say that unless action is taken to remedy this situation, evangelicalism in many quarters may soon be facing a crisis — a crisis of the word. For through their worship practices many churches are unwittingly fettering the word. Strangely, words in themselves abound — whether 'prophetic' words from the congregation or 'preached' words from the pulpit. But the word of God as found in Scripture is scarcely allowed to speak. Add to this the fact that there are a large number of people in our churches who have not adopted the personal discipline of daily Bible reading, and for whom therefore Sunday is the only occasion when they hear God's word, and at that in small measure, the seriousness of the crisis begins to be seen.

Bring back the Bible

'Bring back the Bible into our worship' needs to become the slogan in many of our churches which, no doubt unconsciously, have allowed Scripture to be marginalised. We need to remember the words of John Wesley: 'Although there may be chaff in the pulpit, there is always good grain at the lectern'!

For some, bringing back the Bible may involve using a lectionary. The lectionary adopted in the Anglican Alternative Service Book, for instance, is spread over a two year period and seeks to ensure that on Sundays the worshipping community hears as wide a selection as possible from the Scriptures. Every Sunday there are, as we have already noted, three readings appointed — from the Old Testament, the Gospels, and other parts of the New Testament. In addition, a wide range of Psalms is read too. The three main readings are linked by a very broad theme, so that the choice of one 'lesson' suggests the choice of the other two. The first is sometimes called the 'controlling' lesson, inasmuch as it 'controls' the choice of the others. Thus in the nine Sundays before Christmas (an extended Advent season), where the emphasis is on the world's preparation for Christ, the controlling lesson is from the Old Testament; in the period between Christmas and Pentecost, where the emphasis is on the life of Christ, the controlling lesson is from the Gospels; and in the period after Pentecost, where the emphasis is on our life in the Spirit, the controlling lesson is from the Letters, Acts or Revelation. Clearly such a lectionary has much to commend it. The Scriptures are indeed allowed to speak. Furthermore, the Scriptures in their diversity are allowed to speak.

However, the lectionary approach is not the only way forward. For those who prefer to preach sermon series rather than to preach thematically, the alternative is to ensure that the New Testament reading is always balanced by an Old Testament reading, and vice versa. Such an approach is more demanding, because the preacher often has to think carefully which passage might balance or complement another, whereas the preachers who follow the lectionary already have the work done for them, in the sense that the passages have already been given. In addition, the non-lectionary preacher has to ensure that there is a balance within the various sermon series: balance is not achieved if, for instance, most of the preaching is from Paul's Letters! One way of achieving such balance would be a variant on the lectionary, whereby on autumn Sunday mornings there would be a series on an Old Testament book, on spring Sunday mornings a series on a Gospel, and on summer Sunday mornings a series on a Letter or from the Acts or Revelation. Naturally the preacher would also then have to give some thought to the Sunday evenings, to ensure that they in turn balanced the morning sermons. Whatever, let's ensure that the Bible is read — the Old Testament as well as the New. And along with the main Scripture readings, let's ensure that our congregations are familiar with the Psalms too.

Leave it to the Spirit?

So far I have been assuming that preaching is always planned well ahead. There is, however, another approach favoured by Nonconformists, which involves basically 'leaving it to the Spirit'. This was the approach favoured by Charles Spurgeon, who told his students: 'What is the right text? How do you know it? ... When a verse gives your mind a hearty grip, from which you cannot release yourself. ... Wait for that elect word, even if you wait till within an hour of the service. ... Wait upon the Lord, hear what he would speak, receive the word direct from God's mouth, and then go forth as an ambassador fresh from the court of heaven.'[32] Apart from being exceedingly wasteful of time (it can involve a good deal of time simply settling on a text), this approach can also lead to a very unbalanced diet of Scripture. Subjective in nature, it can result in the preacher preaching on a fairly narrow range of passages and/or subjects. Furthermore, it assumes that the Spirit can only guide one week at a time, whereas in fact there is no reason why the Spirit cannot guide pastors when they plan their preaching programme for the coming year.

If the Bible as a whole is to be brought back into public worship, then surely either serious forward planning or the lectionary approach is necessary. In no way does this involve preachers shutting themselves off from the Spirit. Indeed, experience shows how time and time again, God can speak powerfully and relevantly through passages chosen well ahead. And, of course, there is no reason why from time to time preachers cannot set aside the lectionary or sermon series and preach on some passage which, for one reason or another, God has particularly laid on their hearts. But such occasions will be exceptions. The result is that the overall approach will be balanced and that God's people will indeed be feeding on the whole word of God.

Reading the Scriptures — a practical note

My own particular preference is normally to have the main two Scripture passages read together just before the sermon itself. It is good to encourage members of the congregation to be involved in the public reading of Scripture. A husband and wife, for instance, can read the two set passages together. It is often helpful for the worship leader or pastor to mention the couple by name as they come up to read — this facilitates fellowship, particularly in churches where new people are frequently turning up to service.

Sometimes it can be helpful to preface the readings with a short word as to why they have been chosen. For instance, the theme of the sermon can be announced at this point. In this way the congregation can listen more intelligently to the readings, understanding what is binding them together.

In some circles, Anglican in particular, there is a tradition of concluding each reading with the formula, 'This is the word of the Lord,' to which the congregation respond, 'Thanks be to God.' Less acceptable is the ending, 'May the Lord *add* his blessing to the reading of the Word.' As William Maxwell points out: 'The blessing is in the Word; why therefore pray for it as an addition?'[33]

4

Celebrating the Lord's Supper
— the climax to worship

The centrality of the Lord's Supper

'There is general acceptance of the fact,' writes Ronald Jasper, 'that the eucharist is the central act of worship in the Church. . . . The Free Churches are prepared to admit that it is wrong to regard the eucharist as an infrequent "extra" service.'[34] He then goes on to quote two Baptists, Ernest Payne and Stephen Winward, who stated: 'It is a departure from apostolic worship to celebrate the Lord's Supper infrequently, or to regard it as an appendage.'[35]

There are strong scriptural grounds for such an assertion. Paul's teaching on the Lord's Supper (1 Cor 11:17–34) is given in a context where he is speaking of what takes place when the Corinthians 'come together as a church' (1 Cor 11:18). Likewise, in Acts 20:7, it would appear that, at Troas at least, the Lord's Supper was celebrated once a week: 'On the first day of the week,' records Luke, 'we came together to break bread.' Furthermore, Acts 2:46 would seem to imply that for the Jerusalem Church 'breaking of bread', when presumably the Lord's death was remembered, was a daily occurrence. On the other hand, in all fairness it needs to be recognised that it is highly unlikely that the Lord's Supper was celebrated on every occasion the early church met. C.F.D. Moule rightly makes the point that 'there is certainly nothing to prove that the worship in 1 Corinthians

12 was specifically eucharistic' and goes on to say that 'the non-sacramental meeting for thanksgiving and for prayer, for Bible study and mutual edification must have been as natural and as common then as now'.[36]

Unfortunately the Lord's Supper is yet to become truly central to most Baptist worship. Baptists, for all their desire to honour Scripture and follow its teaching, are for the most part non-sacramental in their worship. The Lord's Supper is normally not celebrated every Sunday — among British Baptists it is generally twice a month, and among other Baptist groupings it is even less frequent. Indeed, among some American Baptists the Lord's Supper is celebrated only once a year — on Maundy Thursday! Poor talkative Baptists! Maybe they need to take note of John Calvin, who regarded infrequent communion as 'an invention of the devil'. Certainly, J.J. von Allmen is of the decided opinion that 'the absence of the Eucharist shows contempt for grace'.[37]

Baptist worship — and much independent worship too — needs to be reformed. The Lord's Supper needs to have its rightful central place. In this way we do what the Lord commands. In this way we focus more regularly upon the centralities of the faith. In this way we have an opportunity to feed by faith on the Lord Jesus and draw strength for the week that lies ahead — an important opportunity when, for various reasons, the sermon has been directed at others and not met our needs.

There is a temptation at this point to discuss the meaning of the Lord's Supper at length. Clearly theology is important, for it is theology which often determines practice. However, as the concern of this book is more practical than theological, we shall concern ourselves first with how we order a communion service, dealing with theological considerations only as they arise from the practice.

Celebrating the Lord's Supper

Let us look at a specimen order of service:

Opening Worship (praise and confession)
SCRIPTURES and SERMON
Prayer/hymn of response
Reception of new members
Song of fellowship
Greeting of one another
INVITATION TO THE TABLE
SCRIPTURE (including Words of Institution)
PRAYER OF THANKSGIVING
BREAD and WINE
Prayers/songs of praise
Prayers for one another
PRAYER OF COMMITMENT
HYMN OF TRIUMPH
THE GRACE

Some elements of the communion service itself have been written in capital letters. These are the items which are essential, however brief the service might be.

It is interesting to compare this order with the ecumenical Lima document on *Baptism, Eucharist and the Ministry* (pages 15–16):

The eucharistic liturgy is essentially a single whole, consisting historically of the following elements in varying sequence and of diverse importance:
— hymns of praise
— act of repentance
— declaration of pardon
— proclamation of the Word of God, in various forms
— confession of faith (creed)
— intercession for the whole Church and for the world
— preparation of the bread and wine
— thanksgiving to the Father for the marvels of creation,

> redemption & sanctification (deriving from the Jewish tradition of the 'berakah')
> — the words of Christ's institution of the sacrament according to the New Testament tradition
> — the 'anamnesis' or memorial of the great acts of redemption, passion, death, resurrection, ascension and Pentecost, which brought the Church into being
> — the invocation of the Holy Spirit ('epiklesis') on the community, and the elements of bread and wine. . . .
> — consecration of the faithful to God
> — reference to the communion of saints
> — prayer for the return of the Lord and the definitive manifestation of his Kingdom
> — the Amen of the whole community
> — the Lord's prayer
> — sign of reconciliation and peace
> — the breaking of the bread
> — eating and drinking in communion with Christ and with each member of the Church
> — final act of praise
> — blessing and sending

Although some of the language may be strange, in fact we shall see that almost all the elements of the 'eucharistic liturgy' as defined in the Lima document are present in the first specimen order. The exceptions, not surprisingly, relate particularly to the solemn preparation of bread and wine and the calling down of the Holy Spirit upon them. The creed may not feature, but we should not forget that in non-conformity we frequently confess our faith in our hymns. Furthermore, in an earlier chapter I have sought to argue that prayers — whether at the beginning of the service or indeed as part of the prayer of thanksgiving for the bread and wine — should be credal in nature. Here too we may look forward to the return of our Lord and to the 'definitive manifestation' of his kingdom. Again, as far as the declaration of pardon is concerned, I have already argued that we should not be afraid of allowing Scripture — as distinct from a priestly figure — to assure the pentitent of forgiveness in Christ. Finally, in some nonconformist circles it may not be traditional to refer to the communion of saints — and yet surely the Lima document is right to remind us that around the Lord's Table heaven and earth do become one in worship, and thus we are bound together with loved ones who have died in Christ.

Let us now go through the specimen order of service.

The opening worship

The Lord's Supper is part and parcel of the main worship of the church. Twenty or more years ago, English Baptist churches had an unfortunate custom of making the Lord's Supper into an optional extra service tagged on to the main service — and often attended by only a few. The reason for the separation between the main service and the communion service was to ensure that the table was 'fenced' and that only committed Christians took the bread and wine. (In this respect, it is interesting to remember that the Roman Catholic word for the Lord's Supper, the 'mass', comes from the Latin *mittere*, meaning 'to send', and refers to the time when the unbaptised were sent away before the Lord's Supper was celebrated. The Lord's Supper was a mystery to be reserved for initiates only). However, such a 'fencing' resulted in many Christians regarding the service as an optional extra, rather than as central to the morning's worship.

To celebrate the Lord's Supper is to celebrate the Lord's Supper with others. Always a corporate event, it presupposes the gathering together of at least the 'two or three'. There is no good reason for an 'individual' communion service. Even a hospital communion can become a shared experience — either with other patients, or with loved ones around the bedside, or with one or two members of the church who have come along with the pastor for the occasion.

Although the Lord's Supper belongs primarily to Sunday worship, there seems to be no good reason to restrict it to one of the main services of worship. There is much to be said, for instance, for a home group celebrating the Lord's Supper together. Church discipline might require the church leadership being informed, but — from a nonconformist viewpoint at least — the pastor need not be present.

The Scriptures and the sermon

Just as at the Last Supper there would have been a solemn recitation of the events leading up to the first Passover and of how God had freed his people from bondage (the Passover *haggadah*), so when the first Christians gathered to break bread and to drink wine, they would have recited the story of how God in Christ had set his people free. This is what is behind the words of Paul: 'For whenever you eat this bread and drink this cup, you proclaim the Lord's death until he comes' (1 Cor 11:26). It is not eating and drinking which proclaim, but the actual telling of the story of our salvation. If, then, we are to continue to 'proclaim the Lord's death' in this context, then this means that the Lord's Supper must always presuppose the preaching of the word. At every celebration of the Lord's Supper, there must always be an opportunity for the word to be proclaimed. This may involve a full thirty-minutes sermon — alternatively it may simply involve a brief five-minutes exposition. A lengthy sermon would not be appropriate at a home communion or an Easter sunrise communion service. But however long or short, the word should always be present. In the words of J.J. von Allmen, without the preaching of the word 'the Eucharist would not be the crown of the cult (ie, the service), but at best an unexplained mystery and at worst a magical act'.[38] A communion service without the preaching of the word is unnaturally truncated.

In the specimen order of service, the Lord's Supper is celebrated after the sermon. It is the moment when worshippers are enabled to respond to the love of God — the love of God as expounded in the Scriptures and as demonstrated in the breaking of bread and the pouring out of wine. A wise pastor will create the service so that the Lord's Supper is the climax to all the worship that has gone before.

Needless to say, the Lord's Supper doesn't just 'happen' to become the climax. The mere fact that the Lord's Supper comes at the end of the service does not guarantee it being the highpoint — it can just as well be an addendum, if the sermon is not seen to link clearly with the Supper. By this I do not mean that every sermon at communion has to centre around the cross. On the other hand, it does mean that every communion sermon has to say something about the grace of God and our need to respond to it. What a wonderful constraint!

To guard against the Lord's Supper becoming an endpiece and nothing more, some worship leaders have sought to centralise it by celebrating it earlier within the service, before the sermon. However, to allow the Lord's Supper to precede the sermon is a theological nonsense and in effect turns the service on its head. For the Lord's Supper is the congregation's opportunity to reflect upon and in turn make it's response to the grace of God. A sermon to follow then becomes very much an optional extra, with the result that the service ceases to have a logical flow.

Reception of new members

Precisely because it is at the Lord's Table that we most sense our oneness in Christ, Baptists have traditionally welcomed new members into the fellowship at the Lord's Supper. There is no one way in which this is done. The new members may have been baptised just beforehand. Alternatively, the new members may be transferring their membership from another church. The larger the church, the more important it is to ensure that the church knows to whom it is committing itself. This should have already happened at the Church Meeting, where the application for church membership has presumably been approved. But, in a large church there are often members at the Church Meeting who will have no idea whom they are approving. Introductions are therefore essential.

Many churches use the occasion to remind the new members of the responsibilities and privileges of church membership. Payne and Winward suggest that a selection of the following scriptures be read: Matthew 10:32; Mark 8:34–35; John 13:33–34; Acts 2:42; Romans 12:4–6; Romans 12:9–13; Galatians 5:22–23, 25; 6:2, 6, 9, 10; Ephesians 4:1–6; 5:25–27, and Hebrews 10:23–25.[39] The way, however, in which these scriptures are often used is to remind the new members of *their* responsibilities, whereas perhaps it is more important to remind the church of *its* responsibilities to the new members. For in accepting new members, the church is committing itself to love, care for and stand by their new brothers and sisters in Christ, whatever.

Formal expression of the church's welcome is normally given in the extending of the 'right hand of fellowship'. This custom, which presumably traces its origin back to Galatians 2:9 ('James, Peter and John ... gave me and Barnabas the right hand of fellowship when they recognised the grace given to me') emphasises the solemnity of the 'covenant' which has been entered on. Just as a business deal can be agreed by shaking hands on it, so the pastor or church leader, on behalf of the church, shakes the new member by the hand in token of the mutual covenant that has been made. In view of the seriousness of this act, the more recent custom of informally putting an arm around the shoulder of the new member may perhaps be questioned, for although a loving gesture, it fails to get to the heart of what is taking place.

Naturally prayer will also be part of the proceedings, as the new members are committed afresh to the grace of God.

In most churches it has been customary for the pastor to say this prayer, but there is no reason why it should not be offered by one of the deacons or church members. There is much to be said for following the prayer with a simple song in which the fellowship expresses its love for one another.

Greeting one another at the Table

At some stage within any worship service, an opportunity should be given to the congregation to greet one another. Of course, such a greeting is not dependent on the Lord's Supper, but it seems appropriate to offer it then as we remember the one who broke down 'the dividing wall of hostility' and has made us 'one' (Eph 2:15). In the early church, the first Christians greeted one another with the 'kiss of love' (1 Pet 5:14; see also Rom 16:16; 2 Cor 13:12; 1 Thess 5:26). Although this form of greeting is perhaps no longer part of our normal culture (at least as far as men greeting men are concerned!), the underlying concept is important. Interestingly, J.B. Philips in his translation of the New Testament rendered 1 Corinthians 16:22 in the following way: 'I should like you to shake hands all round as a sign of Christian love'!

Love needs to be expressed in a concrete act of welcome. The question is, how can we express that welcome today? The Church of England, through its *Alternative Service Book*, has revived the ancient practice of The Peace in which members of the congregation are encouraged to greet one another with the words 'the peace of the Lord be always with you', to which the reply is made 'and also with you'. Personally I have always found this practice somewhat stilted and unnatural, and have preferred to encourage people to get up out of their pews and greet one another in the way and with the words that seem appropriate to them — whether it be a handshake or an embrace, a simple word of greeting or a more enthusiastic word of love.

Ideally, this time of greeting should be the occasion when

those who, for one reason or another, have been out of fellowship with one another, reaffirm their relationship in Christ. For only where relationships are right is worship acceptable. In this respect, Jesus' teaching in Matthew 5:23–24 comes to mind: 'Therefore, if you are offering your gift at the altar and there remember that your brother has something against you, leave your gift there in front of the altar. First go and be reconciled to your brother; then come and offer your gift.' Although Jesus is not referring primarily to the Lord's Supper, the underlying principle makes the passage relevant: a precondition for worship is right relationships. This was a major issue for Paul in his dealings with the church at Corinth. Indeed, he goes so far as to say, 'Anyone who eats and drinks without recognising the body of the Lord (ie, the church) eats and drinks judgement upon himself' (1 Cor 11:29). However, ideals are not always practicable. Relationships cannot normally be restored within a matter of minutes. Far better for a church member to abstain from communion rather than indulge in cheap reconciliation.

The giving of the invitation

At some stage within the service, an invitation to the Lord's Table needs to be given. In many Baptist churches, the church secretary gives the invitation as part of the 'notices'. However, it may be preferable to link the invitation more closely to the communion service itself.

The question arises: who is invited to receive the bread and wine? In many Baptist churches the invitation is extended to 'all those who love the Lord Jesus'. But isn't that a little too vague? In churches which practise infant baptism and confirmation, participation at the Lord's Supper is normally dependent on the individual having been baptised and confirmed. In Strict Baptist churches, participation at the Lord's Supper is normally dependent on the individual having been baptised as a believer. But in most Baptist churches nothing more is demanded than a 'love' of the Lord Jesus — baptism and church membership seem to be quite irrelevant as far as the Lord's Supper is concerned.

But is that right? If people truly love the Lord Jesus, then surely they will want to obey his commands (Jn 15:14) — and not least his command to be baptised (Matt 28:19–20). Clearly, it would be wrong for any church to become more exclusive than Jesus himself and to demand more of people than he would ever have demanded. On the other hand, there is a danger that the term 'love' loses its 'bite' if it is devoid of implications. Thus, if we truly love Jesus, we will want to love his people and commit ourselves to them through the process of their becoming church members. Not to do so is tantamount to not 'recognising the body of the Lord', and thus runs the risk of eating the bread and drinking the wine 'in an unworthy manner' (1 Cor 11:27–29).

The conclusion must surely be that a totally 'unfenced' table, with no restrictions whatsoever, where all and sundry may receive, is not in the spirit of the New Testament. The Lord's Supper is for the Lord's people, and the Lord's people by definition will be those who have publicly committed themselves to the Lord and his people. In Baptist terms, this will mean that the Table is open to those who have been baptised as believers and have become members of their local church. However, in so far as the Lord's Supper is for the Lord's people — and not just for Baptists — in these days of divided understanding on the biblical doctrine of baptism we cannot restrict the Table just to Baptists and others who have been baptised as believers, but rather include all those who are in good standing with their local church, whatever that might mean. This still does not mean that the Table is open to all and sundry. For those brought up within a Baptist context, church discipline needs to be exercised: the normal precondition for participation in the Lord's Supper is baptism and church membership. How is all this reflected in the invitation? Precision, unfortunately, leads to complexity. Perhaps the simplest way forward is to invite all those 'who love the Lord Jesus and have confessed their faith in him'. The wording of the invitation is still inadequate, but at least it points in the right direction.

One strange custom which is gaining ground in some churches is encouraging the children of the church to receive at least the bread, if not the wine. From a Baptist point of view, this is a theological nonsense. The Lord's Supper is for those who have committed their lives to Christ. Inevitably baptism (or in other traditions confirmation) is presupposed. To encourage children to participate in the Lord's Supper, and yet at the same time to believe them not ready for baptism (or confirmation) is illogical.

It is important that the invitation is not worded in such a manner that it gives the impresssion that only those who have reached the right 'standard' may be admitted to the Table. As all pastors know, there are those who fail to take communion because they do not feel 'worthy' enough on a given occasion. The fact is that none of us are ever 'worthy'! Indeed, the moment we feel that we are worthy, we are not worthy enough to participate at the Lord's Table. The Table is for sinners only — albeit penitent ones. This fact needs to be hammered out time and again. In this respect some of the more liturgical invitations are helpful. I frequently use the following formula:

> Come to this sacred table, not because you must but because you may; come not to testify that you are righteous, but that you sincerely love our Lord Jesus Christ, and desire to be his true disciples; come, not because you are strong, but because you are weak; not because you have any claim on heaven's rewards, but because in your frailty and sin you stand in constant need of heaven's mercy and help.

These words can be followed by those Hebrews 10:19–22 —

Therefore, brothers [and sisters!], since we have confidence to enter the Most Holy Place by the blood of Jesus, by a new and living way opened for us through the curtain, that is, his body, and since we have a great priest over the house of God, let us draw near to God with a sincere heart in full assurance of faith.

The reading of Scriptures

Before reading the Words of Institution (1 Cor 11:23–26) themselves, it is helpful to include a selection of other scriptures. Clearly, flexibility is the order of the day. Scriptures may well be chosen with the preceding sermon in mind. Scriptures that are often used include Psalms 116:12–14, 17; Isaiah 53; Matthew 5:6; John 3:16; 6:35; 1 Timothy 1:15; 1 John 4:9–10. Normally the one presiding at the Table will choose the scriptures. On the other hand, in an informal setting members of the 'congregation' can be invited to share words of Scripture which seem to them particularly meaningful and appropriate. The importance of brevity and clarity then needs to be emphasised.

The prayer of thanksgiving

Traditionally Baptist churches have varied as to whether there is one prayer of thanksgiving or two. On 'scriptural' grounds, two might appear best, since our Lord is recorded as having given thanks twice. In fact, if Jesus and his disciples observed the normal Passover routine, there would have been four prayers of thanksgiving! Increasingly, Baptist churches are patterning themselves on the observance of the more liturgical churches and tend to have only one prayer of thanksgiving. In so far as the 'meal' element of the Lord's Supper has fallen away, there is much to be said for this trend.

However, where most Baptist churches differ from many other churches is that normally this prayer is taken not by the pastor but by one of the deacons. This custom derives from their desire to emphasise that Christians need no priest to consecrate the elements. For a similar reason, Baptists remain in their seats to receive communion, to emphasise that they have no altar and therefore no separated priests. By serving one another in their pews, Baptists — along with many other Free churchmen — emphasise the doctrine of the priesthood of all believers!

Michael Walker, an unusually 'high' Baptist, argued against the practice of deacons praying on the grounds that 'the great prayer at the Lord's Table should be offered by the one whom the church has called to be minister of word and sacrament. It makes little sense to call a man or woman to that ministry and then, as a matter of principle, to appoint someone else to offer the church's central prayer'.[40] But this is to misunderstand the nature of pastoral ministry — which is to lead God's people, to teach them from God's word, and to equip them for service. From a New Testament point of view, it is hard to argue that only pastors may administer baptism and the Lord's Supper. True, it may be natural for the pastor to preside at the Table, but this does not debar others from praying at the Table.

Theologically there is nothing against the present Baptist custom, and indeed much to be said for it, if it helps to crystallise the principle that all are equal before God. However, in practical terms this custom of deacons leading in prayer can result in the great eucharistic prayer of the church becoming something of a mixed bag. Instead of focusing above all on the Lord Jesus, the prayer sometimes includes a host of additional items: eg, often the sins of the congregation are confessed afresh (the deacon concerned apparently being oblivious to the fact that earlier on in the service the pastor has already led the congregation in a prayer of confession), and the needs of the fellowship are mentioned before God (the deacon concerned forgetting, perhaps, that a 'pastoral' prayer is yet to come). Although it is true that liturgical niceties are not the be-all-and-end-all of worship, for me at least it does detract from worship when the communion prayer is not primarily Christocentric. In making these criticisms I am not arguing that the pastor should take over the great eucharistic prayer, rather that from time to time instruction is given to deacons on what is required of that particular prayer.

The Lima document assumes that the prayer of thanksgiving will be patterned on the Jewish *berakah* used at the Passover, where thanksgiving is made for the marvels of creation, redemption and sanctification. Our Lord would probably have used this prayer at the Last Supper as he broke bread: 'Blessed art thou, O Lord our God, who bringest forth fruit from the earth. Blessed art thou who hast sanctified us with thy commandment, and enjoined us to eat unleavened cakes.' However, to believe that such a prayer is the essence of the great prayer of thanksgiving at the Lord's Supper seems to be a strange form of liturgical fundamentalism. The focus should surely be on Jesus. The first eucharistic prayer of the Anglican *Alternative Service Book* hits the right note as it offers thanksgiving in the following manner:

> It is indeed right, it is our duty and our joy, at all times and in all places to give you thanks and praise, holy Father, heavenly King, almighty and eternal God, through Jesus Christ your only Son our Lord.
> For he is your living Word; through him you have created all things from the beginning and formed us in your own image. Through him you have freed us from the slavery of sin, giving him to be born as man and to die upon the cross; you raised him from the dead and exalted him to your right hand on high. Through him you have sent upon us your holy and life-giving Spirit, and made us a people for your own possession.

Here indeed is a prayer to emulate! Difficulties arise, however, in the way in which the prayer proceeds, for a little later on the president at the Table says, 'Accept our praises, heavenly Father, through your Son our Saviour Jesus Christ; and as we follow his example and obey his command, grant that by the power of your Holy Spirit these gifts of bread and wine may be to us his body and blood.' What precisely do these words mean? No doubt the language has been chosen to mean various things to various people. Any implication that the bread and wine actually become the body and blood of the Lord is to be rejected. I have no difficulty with the *epiklesis* (the calling down of the Holy Spirit) when it applies to people, but cannot accept the theology which applies it to things. Interestingly, the Anglican New Testament scholar C.F.D. Moule makes the point: 'An "epiclesis" or invocation of the Holy Spirit *upon non-personal objects* is alien to the New Testament doctrine of the Holy Spirit and of persons, and is a retrograde step. Non-personal objects may be consecrated, ie, dedicated for a special purpose in the service of God, but not inspired (2 Timothy 3:16 is exceptional).'[41]

The bread and wine

The traditional Free Church use of small cubes of bread and small individual cups of grape juice seems strange to those of other traditions. It was the Free churches' emphasis on total abstinence which led to non-use of alcoholic wine, which in turn made many feel that small cups are more hygienic. However, if the truth be known, the use of small glasses was due more to advertisers than to doctors. Earlier Baptists shared a few large cups and thereby emphasised the fellowship with the Lord and with one another in the shared cup (see 1 Corinthians 10:16). The same considerations apply to the bread: hygienic scruples have led to the serving of small pieces of bread, but Paul assumes the use of a single loaf, symbolising Christ and his church (1 Cor 10:17).

It is amazing how much passion the issue of the cup — whether a chalice or small individual cups, and the bread — whether one loaf or small cubes, can arouse within a church meeting! Some churches have moved over to using one loaf, but the vast majority still operate with individual cups — and perhaps in this era of Aids are all the more likely to do so.

Maybe this kind of compromise is in fact the way forward. Certainly, the use of individual cups makes the operation of serving communion much speedier.

In this area of the serving of the bread and wine, a whole host of questions involving fine detail arise. Is the bread eaten as it is received, or is it retained until all have been served? Likewise, where individual cups are used, does the congregation wait until all have been served before drinking the wine? In many churches the bread is eaten as it is received, as a sign that we need to come one by one to the foot of the cross; while the wine is drunk together as a sign of the church's oneness in Christ. If, in fact, this procedure is adopted, then there is no reason why the wine cannot be served while the bread is still being distributed. Clearly, more servers will be needed (do they always need to be deacons?). There can, however, be real advantages at times, especially where a large congregation is concerned. And time can be of the essence, not least during the morning service.

Then there is the question of who serves whom. Is it a matter of deacons serving the members of the congregation, or should members of the congregation be encouraged to serve one another actively, using such phrases as 'the body of Christ was broken for you', and 'the blood of Christ was shed for you'? If the latter procedure is followed, it is good to personalise the offering of bread and wine by adding the Christian name of the person concerned: 'the body of Christ was broken for you, Mary'. Such a procedure is demanding — it demands that we know who is our neighbour. But to be named by name at communion can give greater depth to the whole service and prove a most moving experience.

Another set of questions arises which have to do with whether or not there is music while the bread and wine are received. Clearly, there is no one 'right' answer. Personally I prefer the compromise solution: silence while the bread is distributed, but music while the wine is being served. It is, however, important that whatever music is played or sung should help to focus the attention of the worshippers on the Lord Jesus. A virtuoso rendition of a Chopin prelude, for instance, would detract from the service! If the congregation is to sing while the wine is served, then let them sing something which is simple and familiar, and above all cross-centered.

Prayers and songs of praise

The traditional Free Church communion service has been as cheerful as the morgue! The emphasis has been on remembering Jesus and his cross (see 1 Corinthians 11:24–25: 'Do this in remembrance of me'), and so in our mind's eye we have rightly looked back and seen Christ hanging on that cruel cross, a pain-wracked victim bearing the sins of the whole world. However, such an emphasis, though important and vital, can become one-sided. For around the Table we are called not just to look back to the Christ who died, but to encounter the Christ who rose from the dead. Nonconformists may not believe in the Roman Catholic doctrine of the real presence of Christ, and yet, as the Emmaus couple discovered, Christ can be truly present in the breaking of bread (Lk 24:30–31). Furthermore, this risen Lord Jesus has promised to return again in glory: indeed, he calls us to 'proclaim the Lord's death until he comes' (1 Cor 11:26). The Lord's Supper is in fact an anticipation of the Marriage Supper of the Lamb (see Matthew 26:29), when there shall be an end to suffering and to death; when we shall be reunited with our loved ones and all God's people; and when, above all, we shall be united with God himself (Rev 21:3–4). What a cause for celebration!

How can this note of celebration be blended with the serious and sombre task of remembering? The cross cannot be isolated from the resurrection, nor the resurrection from the cross. One way to encourage the note of celebration, albeit in a muted and thoughtful way, is to give the congregation opportunity to express worship after receiving of bread and wine. All too often, almost immediately after the elements have been served, the service is brought to a hasty end, with little if any time allowed for the necessary journey from the cross to the resurrection and beyond. Time needs to be made for worship to build up and come to a climax. The congregation needs to be encouraged to artic- ulate worship in short prayers of praise and thanksgiving — for Jesus. These prayers can be intermingled with worship songs, where the transition is made from love to commit- ment to triumph. This will take time — but it is time well spent. Far better to reduce the time of worship at the beginning of the service, so that there is time to worship the Lord in response to all he has done for us in Jesus.

Preparation is vital if this kind of worship is to flow well. The musicians — whether organist, pianist or worship group — need to know what music is likely to be required. The wise pastor will have chosen a number of suitable songs — and yet at the same time be sufficiently flexible to omit some and incorporate others. Normally such songs will be both simple and well known — the kind of song that many people can sing with their eyes focused on Christ rather than on the songbook! Alternatively, an overhead projector can be used so that people are saved from looking up songs.

Prayers — for one another and beyond

From praise the people can be led to pray for one another. Traditionally, in many Baptist churches this is the point for the pastoral prayer, where the sick and elderly are prayed for, and other members of the fellowship are remembered. Here the horizontal dimension of the Lord's Supper receives expression. For in coming closer to our Lord, we find that we come closer to one another. This is indeed a good point at which to pray for the fellowship. However, it is good not to have too limited a view of Christian fellowship. The needs of the wider Christian fellowship should also be remembered.

This is the time to remember other local churches, the local association (or circuit or diocese) with its superintendent (chairman or bishop), the theological colleges (staff and students), missionary societies, our sister churches overseas. ... There is, indeed, much to be said for the main prayers of intercession coming at this particular point.

However, as well as praying for those not present, it is good to pray for those present around the Table. An invitation can be given to any who would like special prayer, whether for healing or some other personal concern, to move forward to the Table for prayer by pastor and/or deacons and maybe others too. Rather than having folk moving forward in silence, which can often feel threatening, the congregation could sing a number of worship songs while prayers are being offered. This allows for privacy in the praying and gives confidence to those being prayed for. Although, perhaps because of time, many churches may not feel able to offer such an opportunity for prayer at every service, they could at least offer it on a regular (monthly?) basis. Worshippers need to be encouraged to realise that they are pilgrims called to walk together and not in isolation from each other, and that it is therefore only natural and right to ask for prayer from the people of God. Alas, prayer for individual members of the congregation is often reserved for those 'in extremis', rather than a gift which may be used to benefit God's people at any time.

Prayer of commitment

If the Lord's Supper is to be at all meaningful, then it must end in renewed dedication — it must spur us onwards in our service of Christ. Sometimes at the Lord's Table we read the words of the Psalmist: 'How can I repay the Lord for all his goodness to me? I will lift up the cup of salvation and call on the name of the Lord. I will fulfil my vows to the Lord in the presence of all his people' (Ps 116:12–14). At the Lord's Table, when we drink the cup, we too can pay our vows —

indeed, reaffirm the vows of love and loyalty that we made to the Lord in the waters of baptism. Traditionally, Baptists have not used the term 'sacrament' of the Lord's Supper — no doubt in reaction against some of the magical associations with the word found in certain church traditions. However, it is good to be aware that the Latin word *sacramentum* at one time meant a soldier's oath of loyalty to his emperor. In this sense the Lord's Supper can be sacramental: a moment when worshippers renew their commitment to the Lord who loved them and gave himself for them.

A hymn of triumph

Here the service comes to a tremendous climax — or so it should. Alas, this is far from the case, not least because most hymns in the official 'communion' section are so mournful. Surely, however, a hymn of triumph is needed — a hymn where the risen, ascended and reigning Lord Jesus is to the fore. Jesus is Lord — not of the church but of the world, Lord of history, Lord of time, Lord before whom every knee shall bow and every tongue confess. This is the emphasis necessary if the congregation is to go on its way rejoicing!

The grace

The service comes to an end as the congregation bless one another in the words of the grace. Why not bind hands at this point, reinforcing again the oneness that is ours in the crucified and risen Lord? Even the benediction can be a moving experience!

5

Putting It All Together
— an ordered service

Is order desirable?

In spite of Paul's clear teaching in 1 Corinthians 14:40 — 'Everything should be done in a fitting and orderly way', some people apparently believe that order within a service of worship is undesirable and even unspiritual. They cite such verses as 2 Corinthians 3:17 — 'Where the Spirit of the Lord is, there is freedom', and argue that Spirit-led worship cannot be ordered worship. But that argument is a nonsense! It assumes that the Spirit is only found in the spontaneous. If that were so, then much of Scripture would not be Spirit-inspired, for in the Scriptures both order and carefully thought-out patterns are discernible. Surely the Spirit can be as much at work in the planning stage, as in the leading of the service itself. This does not mean that worship leaders should regard the prepared order of service as the law of the Medes and Persians which cannot be changed. Clearly, there should always be room for flexibility, with freedom to respond to the way in which the worship may develop at one particular moment or another. But there should be order. Indeed, a refusal to draw up an order may in the end result in the congregation following an order. Graham Kendrick puts it this way:

> There have been those who believe that unless a Christian meeting is totally unplanned and spontaneous, that it cannot be

Spirit-led. This belief, however, only results in the subtle emergence of an 'unwritten structure', where people's own habits and favourite songs rise to the surface, and mediocrity and predictability creep in once more.[42]

The fact is that totally unplanned worship, far from being more spiritual, is often a sign of laziness and an unwillingness to use one's God-given faculties in his service. God demands our best — not least in the area of worship. And 'our best' will involve careful preparation. In this respect, Ralph Martin helpfully draws attention to David's refusal to 'offer burnt offerings to the Lord my God which cost me nothing' (2 Sam 24:24), and also to Joshua's admonition 'You cannot serve the Lord' (Josh 24:19) to a people who had become easy-going in their idolotrous ways.

> Put into modern terms these biblical verses stress the seriousness of our worship and the claim it lays upon us to have done with all that is slipshod and flippant — not to say frivolous — in our approach to God and our leading others into his presence. ... The Spirit may be relied on to direct and inspire our praise in such a manner that is acceptable to God, if we are prepared to take the offering of praise with fitting attention to what we are doing and why we are doing it.[43]

In other words, leading worship requires hard work and concentrated thought. It is not what we put together ten minutes before the service; it is an exercise which demands our best in preparation. As John Leach rightly notes: 'Good things rarely happen by accident'![44]

A variety of worship forms

Recognising that order is essential, the next questions which arise may be: is there one order of service more 'spiritual' than another? Is there one form of worship more Spirit-inspired than another? Is the traditional Free Church 'hymn-sandwich' any more or less inspired than the Anglican Prayer

Book? Or are both to be rejected in favour of a Pentecostal form of worship, where contributions from the floor may be more the norm?

I have no doubt what kind of a service I prefer. However, ultimately I have to acknowledge that my preferences are not necessarily any more spiritual than another's. The Spirit can work through any and all patterns of worship. The Spirit cannot be bound — he is a Spirit of infinite variety. Just as there are varieties of gifts, but the same Spirit (1 Cor 12:4), so there are varieties of Spirit-inspired worship forms. To say otherwise is to deny that the Spirit has worked in the past; it is also to deny that the Spirit is at work in most of the church today. There is no one fixed Spirit-inspired worship form.

Certainly, as far as the early church was concerned, there was no one fixed pattern of worship. Thus Paul describes (as distinct from prescribing!) the worship at Corinth in these terms: 'When you come together, everyone has a hymn, or a word of instruction, a revelation, a tongue or an interpretation' (1 Cor 14:26). The situation at Jerusalem was different: there the Christians, as well as meeting in one another's homes, continued to participate in the Temple worship (Acts 2:46). Luke tells us that 'they devoted themselves to the apostles' teaching and to the fellowship, to the breaking of bread and the prayers' (Acts 2:42). It has been suggested that this description in fact gives the basic structure of an early order of service: the sermon ('teaching') was followed by the collection (the Greek word *koinonia* could refer to the giving of money, and was used by Paul to describe his collection for the poor of Jerusalem), and in turn by the Lord's Supper ('breaking of bread'), which culminated in prayers for the fellowship and for others. As for the worship at Ephesus, by the time Paul wrote to Timothy the church there seems to have become fairly institutionalised, for in 1 Timothy 4:13 Paul charges Timothy to devote himself to 'the public reading of Scripture, to preaching and to teaching'. There is therefore no one New Testament form of worship. The New Testament teaches variety.

The diversity of New Testament forms of worship stands in sharp contrast to those of the Old Testament where worship procedures are clearly defined. Great attention is given to such matters as the furnishings of the Tabernacle and Temple. However, as Trevor Lloyd rightly says: 'In the New Covenant, God gives us his Spirit, some principles but few regulations, and the responsibility for Spirit-led judgment in the area of worship.'[45] In this respect, Trevor Lloyd goes on to quote the Anglican Article 34: 'It is not necessary that Traditions and Ceremonies be in all places one, and utterly alike; for at all times they have been divers, and may be changed according to the diversities of countries, times, and men's manners, so that nothing be ordained against God's Word.'

The essential ingredients

Although there may not be one basic order of service, there are a number of ingredients basic to worship. It has often been said that the essential ingredients of Spirit-inspired worship find their roots in the Jewish synagogue and the Upper Room. To the praise and prayer, the Scripture readings and the sermon — all characteristic of the Jewish synagogue — were added the breaking of bread and the fellowship of the Upper Room.

Let's take a brief look at these ingredients:

Praise

The Jewish Talmud states: 'Man should always first utter praise and then prayer.' This thought is possibly reflected in 1 Corinthians 14:26, where a 'hymn' (literally, a 'psalm') heads the list of contributions. From Ephesians 5:18 and Colossians 3:16, with their reference to 'psalms, hymns and spiritual songs', we may deduce that the early church knew variety in its worship right from the very beginning.

Prayer

In the synagogue, praise moved into prayer with the 'Eighteen Blessings', which covered a wide variety of intercessions and petitions. Acts 2:42 suggests that in Jerusalem at least, prayer was a hallmark of early Christian worship. Paul likewise expected the churches he pastored to take intercessory prayer seriously (1 Tim 2:1–2).

Scripture

An essential ingredient of synagogue worship was the readings from the Law and the Prophets. 1 Timothy 4:13 indicates that the early church also made much of Scripture reading. For as Paul, with the Old Testament primarily in mind, says to Timothy: 'All Scripture is God-breathed and is useful for teaching, rebuking, correcting, and training in righteousness' (2 Tim 3:16).

Sermon

The Jews called their synagogues 'houses of instruction'. People gathered together to learn from the word of God. After the Scriptures had been read, they were expounded. Likewise, 'teaching' formed an essential element of Christian worship (Acts 2:42; 1 Cor 14:26). As far as Paul was concerned, the role of pastor was synonymous with the role of teacher (Eph 4:11; see also 2 Tim 4:1). Incidentally, in the worship services of the early church preaching was always for the 'edification' of the Christians (1 Cor 14:26). Evangelism took place outside, perhaps in the market-place (Acts 17:17) or the lecture-hall (Acts 19:9).

Breaking of bread

It was in the context of the Upper Room that Jesus broke bread, poured out wine and said, 'Do this in remembrance of me'. Ever since, the Lord's Supper has been a central act of Christian worship (see Acts 2:42; 20:7; 1 Cor 11:17–34).

Fellowship

In a very real sense the Last Supper was a fellowship meal. This sense of fellowship was fostered whenever the first Christians came together, for when they broke bread, they broke bread within the context of a meal (see 1 Cor 11:17–34). It is not insignificant that Luke describes fellowship as a hallmark of their life together (Acts 2:42: see also 2:46)

All these six ingredients, characteristic of worship in the early church, need to find expression in the worship of today's church, however the service may be ordered.

Putting it all together

Recognising that there is no one God-given way for ordering public worship, how can we order our services so that the worship flows in a logical and balanced manner? We have already looked at various aspects of worship. Now let's look at an order of service. (I would emphasise that the following are just two examples of ordering a service.)

A morning service	*An evening service*
Call to worship	Call to worship
Hymn of praise	Hymn of praise
Prayer of praise/thanksgiving	Prayer of praise/thanksgiving
Prayer of confession	Prayer of confession
The Lord's Prayer	Psalm
Greeting of one another	Songs of worship
Children's spot	Testimony
Songs	Song of thanksgiving
Offering	Offering
Notices	Notices
Scriptures (OT and NT)	Greeting of one another
Prayer for illumination	Prayer concerns
Sermon	Prayers of intercession
Prayers of intercession	Hymn

Hymn
Invitation to Lord's Table
Words of institution
Prayer of thanksgiving
Bread and wine
Pastoral prayer
Hymn of resurrection
The Grace

Scriptures (OT and NT)
Prayer for illumination
Sermon
Prayer of reponse
Hymn of response
Benediction

1) *The call to worship*

Both orders of service begin with a call to worship. Ideally, the congregation should already have begun to 'centre down' and focus on God. The call to worship is the moment when the worship leader calls the congregation to be still and know God. The Scriptures are great resource material for directing the congregation's thoughts to God. With the reading (declamation?) of two or three appropriate verses, the majesty, holiness or love of God can be proclaimed. The congregation is thus given 'fuel' to ignite its praise.

2) *Hymns and songs of worship*

Needless to say, the hymns and songs of worship should link in with the call to worship. It is not helpful to read of the holiness of God and then to sing a hymn of praise to Jesus. The hymn or song should form the congregation's response to the particular revelation of God read in the call to worship.

It is possible to sing a hymn and then lead straight into a song. However, particularly if the hymn is quite long, it is helpful to read another scripture, and thus give the congregation extra encouragement for praise. For the same reason, if the opening hymn is followed by prayer, it is helpful to read another brief passage of Scripture before moving on to a further hymn or song.

3) *Prayers of praise and confession*

We have already dealt with this subject in the earlier chapter 'Giving God the Glory'. One point worth emphasising is that the length of prayer may well vary according to the kind of congregation present. In a morning service, with children present, prayers need to be kept brief: three or four minutes at most. In an evening service the prayers can be longer and include silence — but even then most congregations are not able to concentrate on prayers of any real length.

4) *The greeting of one another*

Again, we have already touched on this subject when looking at the Lord's Supper. As these two orders of service make clear, such a greeting need not be limited to the Lord's Supper. Indeed, there is much to be said for giving people an opportunity to greet one another at every service. Apart from anything else, visitors are assured of a warm welcome!

It is important that the greetings do not unnecessarily disturb the order of service. In the example of the morning service, the moment of greeting comes as the service moves from praise to focus on the children. If anything, the greeting emphasises the sense of family awareness present in the children's spot. In the evening service the greeting comes later on — at an earlier stage it would have disturbed the flow of praise.

5) *The children's spot*

In many churches there is a moment when children are central to the service. This originates from the days when afternoon Sunday School was the norm, and when children had to sit through the whole morning service. Today, however, when children often remain in the service for only twenty minutes or so before going out to morning Sunday School, such a 'spot' is less necessary. There is no justification for the old-fashioned children's address, with its three points and complicated visual aids, especially if children are going to have their own teaching session later on in the morning. On the other hand, the children's spot does have its value: it gives the church an opportunity to recognise that children count, and it gives the pastor an opportunity to relate with the children of the church. The 'spot' should be kept brief — four minutes maximum!

With worship particularly in mind, one important point should be made. The temptation to downgrade worship before the children leave for their Sunday School lessons should be avoided like the plague. The worship should be simple and understandable, but this does not mean that it should be 'childish'. Children should have an opportunity to learn some of the great hymns of the church as well as some of the better modern songs of worship. If songs like 'If I were a butterfly', with its references to wiggly worms and fuzzy-wuzzy bears, become the staple diet of the children's worship, the children will gain a warped understanding of what worship is all about.

6) *The offering*

In both orders of service the offering precedes the notices, and not vice versa. That is deliberate. If the offering comes after the notices, it tends to become a business transaction when the members seek to discharge their responsibilities to the church. But if it comes before the notices, and is received within a context of praise, it becomes an act of worship and not just a collection.

One difficulty experienced by an increasing number of people is where they give their 'tithe' to the church by banker's order. The offering then appears to be redundant. If the offering is simply a matter of giving money, it does indeed become redundant for many. But where it is seen primarily as an offering of all that one has — time and energy, as well as money — it retains real meaning. Paul encourages his readers to 'offer' their bodies as living sacrifices (Rom 12:1). The wise worship leader will encourage the congregation to stand as gifts are presented, and see such a standing as an offering of the week that lies ahead, and not just the money in the bag. This will find expression through the offertory prayer, whether offered by the pastor or one of the stewards.

7) *The notices*

Often regarded as a necessary evil, the notices have had a bad press. Some people consider them as the moment when the church secretary seeks to quench the fire of the Spirit engendered by the congregation's worship. But is that true? Notices, of course, can get out of hand — as any visitor to certain university Christian Union meetings can testify! However, where a weekly printed notice-sheet is handed out to the congregation, the actual notice time can be used for highlighting the more significant meetings, and sharing news of the church family (eg, births, deaths, marriages!). Such notices become more than information — they become fuel for prayer. Hence, in the evening order of service, the appropriateness of putting the prayers of intercession after the notices.

8) *The prayers of intercession*

Prayers of intercession can be made at various points in the service. In the morning order, for instance, the prayers are placed after the sermon. Not every sermon would lend itself to that (an evangelistic sermon, for instance, is best not followed by prayers of intercession), but many will. Furthermore, the sermon can often spark off fresh ideas for prayer.

9) *Hymns and songs*

The key should be variety — both in theme and style. The needs of the whole congregation should be kept in mind, and they will always be varied. Not all hymns should express praise, nor should all hymns express response. Not all hymns should be traditional, neither should the latest songs replace all hymns. It has been said that like the scribe who has become a disciple, a local church should bring out of its treasury of praise 'what is new and what is old' (Mt 13:52)!

10) *The Scriptures and sermon*

For some strange reason, the main Scripture readings are often isolated from the sermon. Far better to link the two together, separated only either by a prayer or a suitable hymn which links the readings to the sermon.

11) *The benediction*

Increasingly among evangelical churches, the grace (2 Cor 13:14) is said together as a formal close to worship. It may be said with eyes open and focussed on particular individuals within the congregation, thus becoming a conscious communal form of blessing. The need for variety, however, will mean that the pastor will sometimes want to close the service with a formal benediction (see, for instance, Numbers 6:24–26; Hebrews 13.20–21).

It is a matter of debate whether the pastor prays on behalf of the congregation for God's blessing (and in which case prays, for instance, that God's grace be with 'us') or serves as a channel of God's blessing (and in which case declares, for instance, that God's grace be with 'you'). Andrew Blackwood is of the latter point of view: 'The benediction is an act of God, in which he bestows his grace upon those who are ready to receive it by faith.'[46] But why should the pastor be exempted from receiving such a blessing? J.J. von Allmen is even stronger in his comments on the need for the worship leader to act in effect as a priest in pronouncing the benediction: 'Those ministers who transform the proclamation into a wish expressed in the first person plural are not showing humility, but sabotaging the liturgy, depriving the faithful of part of the grace which God wills to give them. God has chosen ministers to bring into effect the process of salvation, not to impair it.'[47] But where is the scriptural basis for this? Such an emphasis on the pastor as the supreme channel of God's grace makes an unnecessary and false distinction between the pastor and the congregation: there is much to be said for the pastor, in pronouncing the benediction, to make clear that he (or she) is in as much need of God's grace as any other member of the fellowship.

C.F.D. Moule makes the interesting observation:

> With regard to doxologies, blessings, ascriptions, greetings and the like ... the current habit of almost always using an optative or imperative in translations of such phrases seems to be contrary to the balance of New Testament usage. ... Hebrew and Biblical Greek more often than not omit the verb altogether, but where a verb is supplied, it is as often or not in the indicative (eg, 2 John 3: 'Grace, mercy and peace from God the Father and from Jesus Christ, the Father's Son *will* be with us in truth and love'). ... This suggests that some element of confident affirmation has been lost from worship since New Testament times.[48]

Here is indeed food for thought!

6

Cybernetics
— handling body ministry

God's unfrozen people

In 1964 Mark Gibbs and Ralph Martin wrote their celebrated
book *God's Frozen People*, in which they pleaded the case
for the 'laity' to be allowed to use their gifts in the service of
God. Much water has flowed under the bridge since then.
God's frozen people have increasingly become God's active
people — not least in the area of worship.

There was a time when the pastor did almost everything in
the service. Congregational participation was limited to singing
hymns, saying Amens, and giving money in the collection. A
select few were allowed to take up the offering, while occasionally others might be invited to read the 'lessons' for the day.
The deacons were allowed to pray at the communion table,
while the pinnacle of the church secretary's achievement was to
give the notices. But for the most part, in nonconformist
churches at least, that was as far as it went.

How the situation has changed! True, there are still some
churches where time has stood still and where Rip Van
Winkle would feel at home, but in many churches 'lay'
participation has become the norm. Often the pastor will
only preach the sermon, while a deacon or elder will
be entrusted with the responsibility of leading the worship. Then there is the 'worship group' itself — often an
enthusiastic band of guitar-strumming young people — who

will perhaps lead in an opening time reserved for the singing of modern worship songs. Linked to this may be a period of 'open worship', when contributions are invited from the congregation, whether they be a word of testimony or a word of encouragement, a prayer, a reading or a song. Leading prayers of intercession, reading the Scriptures, even administrating baptism and the Lord's Supper are no longer the exclusive preserve of the pastor. Congregational participation and lay leadership are very much a reality. The thaw has set in. God's frozen people have, in many churches at least, become God's 'unfrozen' people.

This thaw is to be welcomed. Today it feels both strange and unnatural to lead a service of worship without active congregational participation. Worship which involves others in both the planning and the executing is always richer than anything a one-man band can offer. Yet such worship has its dangers. For although there is no one pattern of worship, there are certainly principles which lie behind it. Worship is both a science and an art. It is not sufficient to be gifted in leading worship — such a gift needs to be trained and developed. Ideally, pastors will have received such training and development at theological college; their members, however, will need the pastor's help if their own gifts are to come to mature fruition. In other words, pastors cannot abrogate from their overall responsibility for the church's worship. Involving others in the service will never save a pastor time — in fact it will probably increase the load. Solo ministry is always easier than shared ministry, but it is also far less rewarding.

Body ministry

The term 'Body ministry', often used today, stems from Paul's description of the church in 1 Corinthians 12:27 — 'You are the body of Christ, and each one of you is a part of it.' Through his amusing development of the metaphor, Paul makes it quite clear that we need one another: 'The eye cannot say to the hand, "I don't need you!" And the head cannot say to the feet, "I don't need you!"' (1 Cor 12:21). Body ministry is every-member ministry. All are gifted for service and therefore all are involved. In the first place Paul applies this metaphor of body-ministry to the mutual care and concern which Christians should have for one another: 'If one part suffers, every part suffers with it; if one part is honoured, every part rejoices with it' (1 Cor 12:26). This is the ideal for the kind of life that should go on within a church 'home' or 'fellowship' group. In this context, body ministry is simply another term for that kind of in-depth fellowship which is sometimes called one-anotherness (see Rom 12:5, 10; 15:5, 7, 14; Gal 5:10; 6:2; Eph 4:2; 5:21; 1 Thess 5:11).

However, in the wider context of 1 Corinthians 12–14 the term body-ministry can also be applied to worship. The key text here is 1 Corinthians 14:26, where Paul describes the worship at Corinth in the following manner: 'When you come together, everyone has a hymn, or a word of instruction, a revelation, a tongue, or an interpretation. All these must be done for the strengthening of the church.' This is a description of what we would today call charismatic worship. Gifts of tongues and of interpretation, gifts of prophecy and of praise, all are forms of ministry to one another.

Controversy has raged over the validity of these gifts for today. By and large the controversy over the gifts in general is over: most evangelical Christians are willing to acknowledge that there is no reason why, in principle, the Lord should have withdrawn such gifts. Much more difficult, however, is to discern whether a particular tongue or prophecy or whatever is actually of the Lord. Thus Tom Smail, a distinguished 'charismatic' theologian, is on record as saying, 'Two-thirds of the exercise of spiritual gifts is phoney.'[49] The scriptural injunction to 'test' and 'weigh' everything (see 1 Corinthians 14:29; 1 Jn 4:1) is clearly of vital importance.

Cybernetics and the handling of body ministry

This book is concerned with leading worship. The question arises, but is there need for leadership when worship is 'open' and the 'body' is encouraged to minister to one another? Surely the very nature of such worship is that it is not led from up-front? Such reasoning is fallacious. The fact that worship is 'open' and that all are free to participate, does not lessen the need for leadership — if anything, it increases that need. Open worship should never be a 'free-for-all'. Structure and direction are always needed, otherwise chaos ensues. Liberty is not to be equated with licence. This was the Corinthian error. As Paul said within such a context, 'Everything should be done in a fitting and orderly way' (1 Cor 14:26).

Leadership is therefore needed — to be precise, 'cybernetics', the kind of leadership mentioned in the list of the gifts of the Spirit found in 1 Corinthians 12:28. Unfortunately, because of the way many English translations of the Bible have rendered this verse, this gift of leadership is not always apparent. For the Greek word *kubernesis*, translated in the RSV and NIV as 'administration', is literally the word for 'helmsmanship'. (All credit to the *Good News Bible* which recognises this, and speaks of those to whom is given the power to 'direct'). Such a gift has nothing to do with being a good secretary, but everything to do with leading — or 'steering' — a meeting. 'This is an evocative analogy', writes John Gunstone. 'The leader of the prayer meeting is the man at the helm. The gathering is driven along by the wind of the Spirit, but unless the leader's hand is firmly on the tiller, there is every danger that the ship's course may be deflected by the cross-currents of human emotions and ambitions that move not very far below the surface of the sea over which she sails.'[50]

This gift which needs to be exercised within the context of 'open' worship. The leader, normally the pastor, has the re-sponsibility of leading the meeting, 'steering' it in a certain way as it catches the wind of the Spirit in its sails, and at the same time avoids the dangerous rocks and reefs of self-centeredness below. In practical terms this means that the leader provides a structure, gives direction, encourages participation, and ensures that at no stage the meeting gets out of control.

All this can perhaps be best illustrated by the following 'order' drawn up for a 'celebration', where body ministry is to the fore.

PRAISE:	Songs of worship
	Scripture declaring the character of God (eg, a Psalm)
	Prayer of praise and confession
	Songs and prayers of praise (open)
PROCLAMATION:	Scripture
	'Sermon'
	Reflections/contributions (open)
	Songs/*songs*(open) of response
PRAYER:	Prayer concerns for the fellowship, the wider church, and the world
	Prayer concerns for others (open)
	Prayers (open)
	Personal concerns (open)
	Prayers (open)
	Concluding songs and prayer

It will be immediately noticed that there is a clear *structure* to the meeting: praise, proclamation and prayer are its three constituent parts. Each part is important. The leader's task is to ensure that due attention is given to each part. It is, for example, possible for praise to become so dominant that there is no time for listening to God's word or praying for others. On the other hand, it is equally possible that insufficient time is given for praise. I am not seeking to imply through such a structure that at every meeting for open worship the time is rigorously divided into three equal segments — there may be occasions when it is right to emphasise one aspect to the detriment, as it were, of the other two. What I am seeking to advance is the norm.

Note, too, that having a structure includes a timed process. Meetings for worship should not only have a starting time, but also an ending time. To have a fixed time at which the meeting concludes is not, as some suggest, to run the risk of quenching the Spirit, but simply recognising with Paul that 'the spirits of prophets are subject to the control of prophets' (1 Cor 14:32). Where time is deemed irrelevant, such meetings begin to disintegrate, and become the property of the 'enthusiastic' few.

Secondly, it will be observed from the specimen order of service that *direction* is involved. A good deal of preparation is assumed. Such preparation need not be left in the hands of one person. The pastor might be the overall leader, but this should not prevent others, possibly other members of the leadership team, being drawn into the overall planning of the event and being given responsibility for the 'word' or for the leading of the prayer concerns. All this implies direction — the leadership team will through prayerful discussion have agreed on the direction into which they believe the Lord is leading them. True, there must always be an openness to the unexpected leading of the Spirit. As Colin Buchanan helpfully says:

Structure there should be, yes. A vision of what the event may be, yes. A sense of timing and authority, yes. A readiness to test and discern and steer, yes. But still a praying participating assembly may, in the interplay of its contributions, start to take an unexpected course. We can only observe here that to be sensitive to the Spirit is often to be willing to go with the mind of a meeting, not only willingly, but also with a glad sense that God is doing more than has been expected.'[51]

From direction we move to *encouragement*. In churches which have just begun experimenting with open worship, the leader may well have the important task of encouraging people to contribute and share whatever God has laid on their hearts. However, the leader also needs to recognise that silence need not be an embarassment. Silence can be 'golden' — for an individual it can prove immensely fruitful. On the other hand, total silence in open worship is obviously undesirable. Yet noise for the sake of noise is also undesirable. The leader must encourage the best and most relevant contributions. This is where pastoral knowledge of people concerned can be so helpful: from such visiting the pastor may know what God has been teaching particular people, and as the leader of the meeting may actively seek to draw out such testimony.

Unfortunately there is also need for *control*. In a meeting of any size, you will always find the immature and the unstable, the exhibitionist and the attention-seeking, those who have hobby horses to ride and those who, for one reason or another, wish to take over the meeting. In addition there may be those who fail to see the structure of the meeting, who confuse praise with prayer or prayer with proclamation. Alternatively, there may be those who fail to see the direction in which the praise is flowing — who call out, 'Let's sing number eighty-six,' for no better reason than because it's his or her favourite song (Graham Kendrick calls this 'praise bingo'). The leader will try to steer the meeting with wisdom and sensitivity, on the whole simply 'preferring' one way to another, but at times having to 'refute' a contribution. Such 'refutation' should not be done in public unless clear error is involved. It is far better to speak privately to an individual after a meeting.

One aspect of controlling a meeting for open worship is ensuring that, where appropriate, contributions are weighed and evaluated. For instance, when a 'prophetic' word is shared, the leader should encourage the meeting to reflect as to whether or not God was speaking to them, and, if so, what their response should be. It is significant that in the list of spiritual gifts in 1 Corinthians 12:9, the gift of 'prophecy' is immediately followed by the gift of 'distinguishing between spirits'. Likewise the leader needs to ensure that Paul's guidelines on 'tongues' (1 Cor 14:27) are followed, and that their contribution to the meeting is 'weighed'.

The setting for body ministry

Body ministry in terms of 'one anotherness' is best exercised in small home groups. Body ministry in terms of sharing a 'prophetic' word concerning the direction of the church's life and ministry is ideally exercised within the context of the church meeting. Baptists sometimes need to be reminded that their Church Meetings are not 'business meetings' as such, but rather, as the Baptist Union statement on the church of 1948 put it, occasions 'when as individuals and as a community, we submit ourselves to the guidance of the Holy Spirit and stand under the judgement of God, that we may know what is the mind of Christ'. In other words, the Church Meeting is the occasion when words of wisdom and of knowledge are shared, when words of 'prophecy' are spoken, weighed and discerned.

But what about body ministry in terms of open worship? Is such a style of worship to characterise the life of the church as it meets together on a Sunday, or is it something for 'midweek'? Personal preferences are involved here. But so too are group dynamics. We need to recognise that the larger the group, the more difficult spontaneous participation becomes. Shared worship of the kind described in 1 Corinthians 14:26 is not possible where large numbers are involved. The home group is a much more fitting setting. Alternatively, a midweek meeting where numbers don't exceed 80–100 is a possibility. Clearly, opportunities for congregational participation within a large-scale celebration are also possible, but realism demands that such participation will always be limited.

In conclusion, let me quote some words of Stephen Winward:

Such participation is not without its problems, especially in a large company. Some of those who participate may be inaudible, or long-winded, unhelpful or egotistical. Teaching and correction may well be needed, if such abuses are to be avoided or eliminated. The task of pastors and teachers is to equip God's people (Ephesians 4:12). Taking calculated risks is better than excessive caution. 'Do not restrain the Holy Spirit; do not despise inspired messages. Put all things to the test; keep what is good' (1 Thessalonians 5:19–21, GNB).[52]

7

The Dummy Run
— or who is dedicating whom?

Who is dedicating whom?

What is a dedication service? Is it simply a 'dry' baptism
practised by Baptists on their children — or is it something
different? If the truth be told, there is a good deal of
confusion, not just on the part of non-Baptist churches, but
also on the part of Baptists themselves. The Baptist worship
manual *Praise God* talks of 'infant dedication', the *Baptist
Hymn Book* lists dedication hymns under the heading of
'infant presentation', while the Baptist Basics leaflet on the
subject is entitled 'The blessing of infants and the dedication
of parents'.

Biblical texts can no doubt be adduced for each form of
wording. Those who believe the baby is being dedicated can
point to Samuel's dedication in 1 Samuel 1:27–28. There we
read Hannah saying to Eli: 'I prayed for this child, and the
Lord has granted me what I asked of him. So now I give him
to the Lord. For his whole life he shall be given over to
the Lord.' However, the parallel with a twentieth-century
dedication service is scarcely exact. In my experience nobody ever hands over their child to the Lord in the way in
which Hannah handed over her child. Likewise, as far as the
term 'infant presentation' is concerned, the parallel with the
presentation of Jesus in the Temple (Lk 2:22) is hardly
any more appropriate: sacrifices are not generally held

at dedication services! What's more, this ceremony only applied to the first-born, who were considered to belong to the Lord and had to be 'redeemed' by him. The most helpful parallel is found in the story of Jesus blessing the children (Mt 19:13–15; Mk 10:13–16; Lk 18:15–17), yet even there the parallel is not exact: only mothers seem to have been involved, and the occasion only seems to have been one of blessing, with no act of dedication on the parents' part.

Honesty compels one to admit that there are no biblical grounds as such for this custom. But then there are no biblical grounds as such for weddings and funerals being held in a church! However, just as it seems to us right and proper to mark weddings and funerals by a Christian service, so it is equally right and proper to mark the birth of a child by a Christian service. It is natural to want to thank God for the gift of a child and to ask his blessing on that child. Furthermore, the birth of a child is of such importance that it demands the utmost parents can give, as it also calls for the utmost grace that God can give. In other words, a dedication service is primarily a service of thanksgiving and blessing for the child, and of dedication of the parents.

Dedication within the context of worship

Any parents worth their salt will have thanked the Lord for the gift of their child long before they take the child into the church itself for a service of dedication. Likewise they will have asked God's blessing on their child, and indeed perhaps already have consciously sought God's grace as they committed themselves to their task of Christian parenthood. So what else does a formal dedication service in church have to offer? The public element of the service strengthens both the parents' thanksgiving and dedication. The service also, however, enables the church as a church to be involved. This involvement relates not simply to shared thanksgiving for the new life of the child and prayer for the parents, it also gives the church members an opportunity to dedicate themselves to sharing in the Christian upbringing of the child, whether through Sunday School and the Youth Fellowship, or through the effect that the general ethos of the church has on the child.

There was a time in Baptist life when dedications were relegated to the end of the morning service, after the last hymn, as if they were just an addendum. Today, however, dedications have become an integral part of the main service — in many churches taking the place of the 'children's talk'. By the very way in which the dedication is now placed within the service, the church recognises the importance of Christian family life.

The dedication 'service'

The dedication 'service' itself is made up of a number of components. A typical order would take the following form:

Welcome
Introduction to the purpose of the service
Scriptures
Questions — to parents
           — to congregation
Prayer
Presentation of Bible
Hymn/song

1) *The welcome*

Normally a formal order of service for a dedication includes a welcome to the parents. However, in many ways it is much more important to welcome the friends and relatives, many of whom will have turned up especially for the event. Dedications are often viewed as 'social' occasions, just like many services of infant baptism. Although from a Christian viewpoint a dedication service has a much deeper meaning, there is a lot to be said for encouraging the social element. If a dedication lunch-party will result in more people coming to church before the celebration, then there is everything to be said for the custom. This will mean that the service has evangelistic potential.

A warm welcome therefore becomes important. It is vital that those visiting the church for the first time feel the warmth of the fellowship's love. This will involve not just the pastor giving a warm greeting from the front, but also good stewarding before the service itself. Furthermore, church members need to be on the 'qui vive' after the service and talk to their visitors rather than pursue their own business.

2) *The purpose of the service*

Precisely because there is so much confusion about the meaning of dedication — is it just a 'dry' baptism — it is helpful to spell out briefly what is to happen. For instance:

> In this service of dedication we will first give thanks to God, the maker of all things, the giver of all life, for the creation and birth of this child.
>
> Secondly, we will make a solemn promise as parents and as a church that, relying on God's help and working in partnership together, we will endeavour to bring up . . . in the discipline and instruction of the Lord.
>
> Thirdly, we are to pray that God's blessing may descend and rest upon . . ., remembering how the Lord Jesus took little children in his arms and blessed them, laying his hands upon them.

3) *The Scriptures*

Although there may not be firm biblical precedents for a service of dedication, there are, of course, a good number of biblical principles highly relevant to the occasion. Clearly time is limited and one cannot read every relevant scripture. However, the following three Scripture passages are particularly appropriate:

Deuteronomy 6:4–7 — God-talk is not to be reserved for special occasions, but is for every day.

Ephesians 6:1–4 — Parents and children have mutual responsibilities to one another.

Mark 10:13–16 — If Jesus took children seriously, then so should we!

4) *The questions*

At this stage the pastor should encourage the parents to stand with their child. Ideally they should stand not with their backs to the congregation, but facing the congregation. This is particularly important in a large church, for it gives people an opportunity to put names to faces.

The following question may then be asked of them: 'As you dedicate yourselves to the Lord, do you promise — before God and this congregation — to bring up ... in a Christlike way; to teach him/her the truths and duties of the Christian faith, and by prayer and example bring him/her up in the life and worship of the church?'

At this stage the congregation should be asked to rise, and the members given an opportunity to commit themselves to the family before them (it is unhelpful just to get the members themselves to stand, for otherwise the visitors begin to feel like second-class citizens). The following wording can be used:

As a congregation we too are involved in the Christian up-bringing of. ... In our life together we are called to set an example of love and service. However, in particular I would ask the members of this church to befriend, encourage and pray for this family, so that ... may in due time come to trust Christ as Saviour and confess him as Lord in baptism. If you, the members of this church are so willing, will you signify your acceptance of this responsibility by saying, 'We do'.

5) *The prayer*

It is customary for the pastor to take the baby from the mother, pray for it by pronouncing the Aaronic blessing (Num 6:26) on the child, and then returning it to the father — symbolising that both parents are involved.

In many churches the pastor, after pronouncing the blessing on the child, also prays for the child and its family. An alternative is to involve one or two others in the service and invite them to pray (maybe a couple in the church who are good friends of the family). Where others share in the praying, it is good to ensure that there is a clear understanding of what is involved in the service so that the prayer reflects the overall meaning of the service: thus along with thanksgiving for the child, prayer should be made for the child (looking ahead, for instance, to the day when the child comes to commit its life to the Lord in baptism) and for the parents.

6) *Presentation of a Bible*

One happy custom found in many churches is that of giving a Bible (by the pastor, or by a representative of the Sunday School), to the child for whom prayer has been made. Although the child may be too young yet to read, the presentation of the Bible is a reminder of the hope that the child may indeed come to read God's word for him or herself. In a day when education for so many parents is an all-consuming concern, the church reminds itself and others that 'the fear of the Lord is the beginning of wisdom' (Prov 1:7).

7) *Hymns and songs*

As in a wedding or a funeral, it is often appreciated if the pastor can involve the family concerned in the choosing of hymns and/or songs. Clearly, the words must be appropriate for the occasion. However, it may well be that a hymn the couple had at their wedding might strike the right note of praise for the beginning of a service. Again, they may choose a hymn or song to follow the service of dedication, and which might become a vehicle for the congregation's prayers for the family. The more worship can be personalised on such an occasion, the more meaningful it becomes for the family. Ultimately, however, the pastor must have the right of 'ministerial veto'!

Variations on the norm

In most churches services of dedication are held for one couple at a time. Clearly, however, there can be variations to this norm. In a large church with plenty of young couples there will be plenty of babies. Rather than have a dedication service every other Sunday, it makes sense to involve a group of couples on a given occasion. Again, increasingly in our churches, there are unmarried mothers who wish to have a service of dedication. They too should be welcomed. Where possible, it is nice to hold such a dedication service alongside the dedication service of another family in the church — not only does the unmarried mother feel less isolated, but also a new friendship often develops between that mother and the other family involved. The fact that both families were involved in the same dedication service some-how forms a special bond, which in turn can result in support and encouragement to the unmarried mother.

So far we have assumed that the parents for whom a service of dedication is arranged are committed members of the church. But what about non-believers who wish for such a service? My own rule of thumb is that provided the couple want to take God 'seriously' (this would involve, at the very least, an intention to come along with their child to church on Sundays), then there is no reason why there cannot be such a service of dedication. Of course, the pastor will want to ensure that the parents understand what they are doing — it is not enough for them to want their child 'done'! How-ever, where there is a genuine concern on the part of the parents to go 'God's way', then that should be encouraged. A parallel can be drawn with the marriage service, which too is open to Christians and non-Christians alike: dedication, like marriage, belongs to the order of creation rather than the order of redemption. The service may not have the same meaning as for a Christian, but nonetheless it will still have some meaning.

8

Baptists Are Wet All Over
— *confessing the faith*

Of all the services that take place within a Baptist church, unquestionably the most moving are always the baptismal services. For candidates and congregation alike, worship reaches its highpoint on such occasions. Praise is at its most vibrant, and preaching at its most powerful. A sense of expectancy is present — not only do the candidates look to God to bless, but the congregation itself expects God to work, not least through the preaching of the word. As with Cornelius and his friends, people who have faith are not disappointed, for faith often proves catalytic and the Spirit moves in their midst (see Acts 10:30–48). It is particularly in the context of a baptismal service that many come to surrender their lives to Christ.

An 'in-house' affair or Gospel proclamation?

First, an important question needs to be faced: what precisely is the nature of a baptismal service? This is an important question, for only when we have established the nature of the service can we go on to examine related structures of worship.

As a teenager I belonged to a church where there was a baptismal service almost every month. Those services were devoted to Gospel proclamation — many non-Christians were there, and month after month many of them responded to the Gospel invitation. Normally the baptisms came almost at the end of the service: all that separated them from the closing benediction was the singing of the hymn 'Just as I am, without one plea', before which (and, indeed, during which) appeals were made for people to come forward to receive Christ as their Saviour and Lord.

This tradition of baptism as a time of Gospel proclamation is common to many Baptist churches. But over against this tradition is another tradition, now proving increasingly popular and represented by many books of orders of service. Here the preaching is directed at the candidates rather than the guest: the emphasis is discipleship. No longer is John 3:16 the order of the day, rather such texts as Mark 8:34 ('If anyone would come after me, he must deny himself and take up his cross and follow me') are preferred. Baptism is then no longer the climax of the service. Rather it leads into a celebration of the Lord's Supper, where the candidates are received into membership and admitted into communion.

Theologically, this latter model has much to commend it.

- It emphasises the corporate aspect of believers' baptism. Thus in 1 Corinthians 12:13 Paul wrote: 'We were all baptized by one Spirit into one body . . . and we were all given the one Spirit to drink.' Baptism is the door through which we enter the church. It is a rite of initiation. It ought not to be possible for people to be baptised in a Baptist church without their becoming church members — or at least when it does happen the circumstances should be exceptional (eg, occasionally people from paedobaptist churches wish to be baptised as believers, and yet remain a member of their own particular paedobaptist church). Baptism is a church ordinance — it is not for spiritual gypsies!

- It emphasises the fact that baptism leads to communion. An unbaptised communicant is a theological nonsense. As we have already seen, to break bread and yet not be baptised is tantamount to not 'recognising' or 'discerning' the body (1 Cor 11:28), which according to Paul is to invite judgement on oneself.

In addition, we may mention that this 'in-house' model is in accord with the practice of earlier times. Thus most records of communion services left us from the early centuries of the church are of baptismal eucharists.

On the other hand, the 'Gospel proclamation' tradition has much to commend it too.

- It emphasises that baptism is the moment for confessing the faith. Thus Paul writes to Timothy: 'Take hold of the eternal life to which you were called when you made your good confession in the presence of many witnesses' (1 Tim 6:12). This is why we cannot have private baptisms on a Sunday afternoon — as one of my former candidates once requested. Baptism can never be a private affair. Indeed, it could be argued that modern baptistries are in one sense an unfortunate compromise: a river or lake is much more public!

- On a practical note, with perhaps the exception of Christmas, baptismal services are often the occasion when the church is at its fullest, with a good number of unbelievers present. I, for instance, used to encourage my candidates to make a list of their friends, relatives and enemies — and then invite the lot! Each candidate would often bring along twenty friends to the service, many of them non-Christians. When so many 'pagans' are present, baptismal services can be one of the few occasions when we can genuinely proclaim the Gospel as distinct from teaching the faith.

It is above all for this last reason that, on pragmatic grounds, I favour the old 'Gospel proclamation' tradition. Certainly, if fifty or more unbelievers are present, it really does not seem right to follow baptism with communion.

Confessing the faith

Let us then look at a specimen order of service

	Welcome and notices
PRAISE	Call to worship
	Hymn: Praise my soul the King of heaven
	Prayer of praise and confession
	Scripture: Isaiah 55:6–7
	Song: God forgave my sin
	Offering
PROCLAMATION	Scriptures: John 3:1–16; Acts 19:1–7
	Prayer for illumination
	A 'Gospel' sermon
RESPONSE	Prayer of response
	Hymn: Just as I am, thine own to be
	Scriptures: Matthew 3:13–15; Romans 6:3–4; Matthew 28:18–20
	Song: He is Lord (Baptisers into pool!)
(Proclamation)	Testimonies/Baptisms
CELEBRATION	After each baptism, a song chosen by candidate:
	O Lord you are my light
	Majesty, worship his majesty
	Lord, you are more precious than silver
	I will enter his gates with thanksgiving
	This is the day, this is the day
	I just want to praise you
	When the Spirit of the Lord is within my heart
APPEAL	Invitation
	Hymn: Come let us sing of a wonderful love

AFFIRMATION   Scriptures: Matthew 3:16–17; Acts
                     1:18
                     Giving of a text to each candidate
                     Prayer with laying-on-of-hands

CELEBRATION/
  APPEAL   Hymn: To God be the glory
                     Benediction: Romans 15:13

It is interesting to compare this order with the ecumenical
Lima document *Baptism, Eucharist and the Ministry* which
states on page 6:

> Within any comprehensive order of baptism at least the follow-
> ing elements should find a place:
> — the proclamation of the scriptures referring to baptism
> — an invocation of the Holy Spirit
> — a renunciation of evil
> — a profession of faith in Christ and the Holy Trinity
> — the use of water
> — a declaration that the persons baptized have acquired a new
>   identity as sons and daughters of God, and as members of
>   the church, called to be witnesses of the Gospel.
> Some churches consider that Christian initiation is not complete
> without the sealing of the baptized with the gift of the Holy Spirit
> and participation in holy communion.

It will be seen that, with the exception of communion, all the
above elements are present or implicit in the above order.
Even in the area of baptism, churches are beginning to come
together!

Let us then go through the specimen order of service:

1) *Welcome*

Particularly at a baptismal service, where many guests may
be present, it is important to give them a warm welcome and
make them feel at home. It is good to encourage visitors to
sign special cards as a record of their visit that day. It is so
easy for visitors on such occasions to get lost in the crowd.

Where a card has been signed, a letter of greeting may be sent out to them the following week, assuring them that there would always be a welcome at church! As far as making visitors feel at home is concerned, it can be very helpful to produce a printed order of service so that the visitors can feel secure, knowing that the service, often fairly lengthy on these occasions, has an appointed end!

2) *Opening praise*

Baptisms best take place within the general context of praise. The praises of God's worshipping people form a wonderful sounding-board for the Gospel, as it is proclaimed in the sermon and enacted in baptism.

Traditionally, Baptists have given time to praising the Lord before the baptisms take place, but have then allowed the baptismal service to come to an abrupt conclusion with the baptisms themselves. Normally there was just a concluding hymn after the baptisms, and that was it. This tended to result in a sense of anti-climax. There is much to be said for allowing the baptisms to form a fresh spring-board for the praises of God's people.

3) *The sermon*

As we have seen, baptismal services offer unique opportunities for the preaching of the Gospel. If candidates have really worked at the business of inviting friends and acquaintances, then a large number of people present who normally never darken the door of a church. To fail to preach the Gospel would be to fail them.

Baptismal services are not the moment to major on the fact that Baptists are right, and all the paedobaptists are wrong! This would be to abuse the occasion. Having said that, it is helpful within the overall context of an evangelistic address to explain that baptism is faith's response to God's offer of salvation in Christ.

4) *The baptismal scriptures*

Before proceeding with the actual baptisms, an explanation needs to be offered of what is involved.

In several baptismal orders, statements concerning the meaning of baptism are to be found. Thus Gilmore, Smalley and Walker present the following statement:

> Let us now recall what we understand concerning the benefits promised by our Lord to those who receive believers' baptism and become members of his church.
>
> In baptism we become one with Christ through faith, sharing with him in his death and resurrection, and the washing of our bodies with water is a sign of the cleansing of the whole of our life and personality.
>
> In baptism we mark the receiving of the Holy Spirit, who has brought us to the moment of commitment and who will strengthen us for future endeavour.
>
> In sharing in this act we are obeying the commandments of our Lord, making confession of our personal faith in him, and becoming part of the one holy, catholic and apostolic church.[53]

Personally I prefer to read three baptismal scriptures (Matthew 3:13–15, concerning Jesus' baptism; Romans 6:3, 4, where Paul talks of baptism in terms of dying and rising with Christ; and Matthew 28:18–20, where baptism comes in the context of the Great Commission) as an explanation and justification for the practice about to be followed (again, this is in line with what is suggested in the Lima document *Baptism, Eucharist and the Ministry*). There is no more powerful voice than the voice of Scripture. Let God's word be heard!

5) *Confession through testimony*

Baptism itself is the great testimony to Christ. For it is in baptism that one makes 'the good confession in the presence of many witnesses' (1 Tim 6:17). However, that testimony becomes more meaningful to outsiders when it is further articulated in word. The baptismal service therefore normally incorporates not just an act of confession, but also provides an occasion for confession.

But how does one lead into the testimony? One possibility, advocated by the Scottish Baptist order, is to ask each candidate a question along these lines: 'Would you tell us briefly in your own words, that you believe in Christ, your Saviour and your Lord'. My own preferred approach is to ask two simple questions: 'Which verse of Scripture has been particularly meaningful to you?' 'What has made this text have meaning?' I have found that even the shyest of candidates is able to read a text in public. Then they have found it not so difficult to give a brief (some briefer than others!) answer as to why it has been meaningful. Clearly, the object of the exercise is for candidates to choose a text which relates to their experience of Christ, whether in conversion or possibly subsequently.

Occasionally some people are so nervous that the testimony-giving actually becomes a bar to baptism. Needless to say, this should not be the case. One way round such a difficulty is for the pastor — or one of the people who, on behalf of the Church Meeting, visited the candidate for baptism and membership — to introduce the person concerned and give their testimony on their behalf!

6) *The confession in the pool*

It could well be argued that if the testimony has already been given, then no further confession is necessary. This would appear to be the view of the Scottish Baptists in their order. There the baptiser simply states: 'At your request, and upon your confession of faith in the Lord Jesus, I baptise you in the name of the Father, the Son and the Holy Spirit.'

On the other hand, there is something to be said for the candidate having a further opportunity of clarifying his or her testimony by answering one or more simple questions. I usually ask the following question: 'Do you ... profess repentance toward God and faith in Jesus as Saviour and

Lord?' On receiving the affirmative, I then go on to say, 'Then I baptise you in the name of the Father, the Son and the Holy Spirit.' Somewhat stronger theologically are the two questions suggested in *Praise God*: 'Do you acknowledge Jesus Christ as your Saviour and Lord?' 'Do you promise with the help of the Holy Spirit to serve him in the church and in the world unto your life's end?'[54]

Andrew Leakey, pastor of Red Hill Baptist Church, Worcester, gets his candidates to answer four questions — after each question they take a further step down into the pool!

1) 'Do you turn away from all sin and the temptations of this world, and reject the Devil and all his works?'
2) 'Do you confess Jesus Christ as your Saviour?'
3) 'Do you confess Jesus Christ as your Lord?'
4) 'Do you promise with the help of the Spirit to serve Jesus in his church and the world?'

Although I am not in favour of distingushing between Jesus as Saviour and Lord, there is something to be said for the explicit renunciation of evil (this is in line with the Lima document *Baptism, Eucharist and the Ministry*), as also for the dedication to Christian service. On the other hand, if a number of candidates are involved, four questions a candidate can prolong a service.

As far as the actual practice of baptism is concerned, a number of practical questions arise.

1) *How precisely does one baptise?*

Present-day Baptists agree that baptism is administered to the candidate by immersion. Affusion is a last resort — in the case, for instance, of a person who is physically incapable of being baptised by immersion. For although at the end of the day it is the quality of faith rather than the quantity of water that counts, immersion is the method best suited to symbolise much of the meaning of baptism: eg, dying with

Christ and rising to newness of life (Rom 6:3–4); washing away one's sins (Tit 2:4).

But how is a person best immersed? Traditionally, in Britain, candidates are taken backwards — a sign for us of being buried with Christ. In parts of Africa candidates are baptised by being plunged into the water — a meaningful symbol where people are buried vertically! An alternative mode — especially where large people are concerned — is to have them kneeling in the water and then take them forwards as a sign of their submission to Christ.

2) *Who actually baptises?*

Who baptises the candidates? Is it the pastor who, at least traditionally, has been ordained as a 'minister of the word and sacraments'? Or may others be involved? Interestingly, the more sacramental churches do not restrict the rite of baptism to the priest — provided the correct Trinitarian formula is used, anybody may baptise. Personally I, as pastor, would always want to be involved in the actual process of baptising. However, there is no reason why only the pastor should be involved. Indeed, if the candidates are to be taken back as they are baptised, there is much to be said for someone else — a deacon or a housegroup leader — to share the load.

3) *How many may one baptise?*

Luke tells us that on the day of Pentecost, 3,000 were baptised (Acts 2:41). At the 1990 Baptist World Alliance Congress in Seoul, the Koreans arranged the largest baptismal service in history with some 10,000 being baptised in the Olympic swimming pool!

My own advice is to limit the number of those being baptised at any one time. This is partly for sheer physical reasons — for one person to baptise twelve people in the traditional manner is an exhausting business. It also becomes an exhausting business for the congregation to watch! If large numbers are involved, there comes a stage when the candidates cease to be people confessing their faith and become instead 'bodies' to be 'done'. I believe this 'exhaustion' factor relates not just to the one service, but also to the Sunday itself — I am not greatly enamoured with the practice of holding baptismal services both morning and evening on the same day. It is far better to spread one's candidates out — baptising, for instance, eight one month, and eight another month, rather than sixteen all at one go. It is good to aim to make baptismal services regular (ideally monthly!) events in the life of the church.

7) *The songs of celebration*

Normally, as the candidates are baptised, a verse of a hymn or a song is sung. In more traditional Baptist churches there used to be one baptismal hymn, a verse of which was sung as each candidate was baptised. If there were more candidates than verses, then the congregation would repeat the hymn. Typical hymns were 'O happy day that fixed my choice' or 'Just as I am, Thine own to be'. Alternatively baptismal 'sentences' were sung: eg, 'Be thou faithful unto death and I will give thee a crown of life'. It could all be very solemn.

A more recent — and welcome — trend is to encourage the candidates to choose a short song that is particularly special to them. The very nature of the songs that are chosen, as indicated by the above specimen order, rightly expresses the note of celebration.

Colin Buchanan suggests that the note of celebration might be struck by some kind of festal shout. He writes: 'When an adult (and an infant) comes from the waters of baptism, it is well worth trying an ejaculatory shout, as, for example, the minister to shout out "Praise God for Bill's baptism into Christ", with a response like "Hallelujah. Amen."'[55] Personally I prefer the celebratory songs!

8) *The appeal*

In most Baptist churches a baptismal service is used to challenge others to follow Jesus. However, the precise nature of that appeal varies. In *Praise God* and the Scottish Baptist orders of service, the appeal is seen in terms of challenging others to be baptised. Thus the Scottish order reads: 'Invite any who have been moved by the service to desire baptism to come forward during the baptism, and to shake hands in token of a desire to discuss the matter at an early date.' On the other hand, particularly where the emphasis has been on Gospel preaching, the appeal may be seen as more evangelistic in nature.

There is probably no gain in being too specific. The challenge is to move on to the 'next step'. For some this will be a 'decision for Christ', for others it will be baptism.

Whether or not people are invited to come forward in response to an 'altar call' is immaterial. Theologically, the practice of inviting people to come forward as a 'confession' is dubious — baptism is the moment of confession. On the other hand, it is important that some concrete step is taken. In my own experience there is much to commend asking people to have a word with the pastor, who would then give them either an evangelistic booklet (eg, Norman Warren's *Journey into Life*) or a leaflet about baptism.

The appeal in this particular order is strengthened by a hymn of invitation: eg, the congregation, through the singing of 'Come let us sing of a wonderful love', shares in the giving of that appeal.

9) *The laying-on-of hands*

Many churches have revived the old Baptist practice of baptism being followed by laying-on-of-hands. The custom, of course, is not specifically Baptist, but rather goes back to Scripture. (For early examples of the rite, see Acts 8:17; 19:6.) By the time of the letter to the Hebrews it had become general, at least in the churches known to the writer (Heb 6:2).

Customs vary as to when this rite is carried out. It can take place in the waters of baptism, immediately after the baptism itself. This gives a sense of immediacy. The disadvantage is that the candidate is still recovering from having been dipped under the water. It is probably better to give the candidates time to get changed. This can be done by having a 'buffer' hymn (during which the appeal is given) before going on to pray for them.

As with baptism, so too with prayer-with-laying-on-of-hands, some explanation needs to be given. The introduction of Scripture is helpful. Suitable passages are Matthew 3:16–17 — 'As soon as Jesus was baptised, he came up out of the water. Then heaven was opened to him, and he saw the Spirit of God coming down like a dove alighting on him. Then a voice said from heaven, "This is my own dear Son, with whom I am pleased"', and Acts 1:8 — 'Jesus said, "When the Holy Spirit comes upon you, you will be filled with power, and you will be witnesses for me in Jerusalem, in all Judea and Samaria and to the ends of the earth."'

The purpose of such prayer is to invoke the Spirit to come and fill the candidates with fresh power for service. As the candidates have been baptised in water, so a fresh baptism of the Spirit is requested. Clearly the candidates have already received the Spirit, but now they desire yet more of Him.

Theologically, this ceremony may be viewed as a form of 'lay ordination'. The candidates are being set apart for service. *Praise God*, for instance, has this emphasis in its suggested prayer: 'Bless, O Lord, this your servant. Strengthen him by the Holy Spirit, as we now in your name *commission* him for the service and ministry of Jesus Christ our Lord.'[56] This emphasis is also apparent in the Lima document *Baptism, Eucharist and Ministry*, which states that the calling of the candidates to be witnesses of the Gospel should be publicly declared.

Praise God assumes that the pastor will pray. However, it is far better to involve others: eg, deacons and/or those who have interviewed the candidate for membership. Needless to say, this does not exclude the pastor from being involved!

It is also possible to link this ceremony with the giving of a 'text' to the candidate (written on the baptismal certificate). If this is done, then before prayer is made the 'text' can be publicly given and then woven into the following prayer. Here there is room for creativity and sensitivity in finding words of Scripture that are particularly relevant to the candidates concerned.

It is possible to link this particular ceremony with the formal welcoming of the candidates into church membership. Thus *Praise God* suggests that immediately after the laying-on-of hands, the minister extends the right hand of fellowship, saying, 'In the name of the Lord Jesus Christ, and on behalf of this congregation, I welcome you into membership of this church.'[57] To me this seems something of an anticlimax — the formal giving of the hand cannot compare with the loving solemnity of the laying-on-of-hands. The Scottish Baptist order suggests that before the baptisms the pastor says, 'This service is held, and these friends are welcomed into membership by baptism, in accordance with a resolution of the church taken upon (date . . .). The names of our candidates today are. . . .' The candidates are then subsequently welcomed at the Lord's Table, not 'into membership', but 'to their first communion as members'. The alternative is simply to welcome the candidates into membership at the next communion service.

10) *A final note of celebration and appeal*

From prayer the service turns to celebration and a further appeal. This double aspect is well expressed in a hymn such as 'To God be the glory great things he has done'. Praise and worship is offered through the hymn, and yet an appeal is given through the chorus itself: 'O come to the Father through Jesus the Son'.

9

God Is In The Midst of You
— worship and the unbeliever

Worship can be winsome

My initial approach to worship and evangelism was somewhat negative. The two, in my opinion, did not belong together. In taking this line I was much influenced by my experience of evangelism while a student at Cambridge. There, in my day at least, every Sunday evening at 8.30 we had the CICCU (Cambridge Inter-Collegiate Christian Union) Sermon. This consisted of a hymn, a prayer, a Scripture reading, the sermon, a prayer of response and a closing hymn. All the emphasis was on the sermon — everything else was secondary. Students were invited to hear the word preached. This particular method of evangelism proved most successful: year by year literally hundreds of young men and women surrendered their lives to Christ.

Not surprisingly, when later I became a pastor, I took the CICCU Sermon as the model for my evangelism. At the Guest Services we held, the sermon was paramount. I sought to eliminate as much as I could of the normal worship service: prayers of intercession went out of the window, and hymn-singing was cut down to a bare minimum. I argued that if the service was to be aimed at the outsider, then as much as possible of the service should make sense to the unbeliever. Hard-headed proclamation without the trimmings was the aim. If I had a scriptural model, then it was to be found in Luke's description of Paul's approach to

117

evangelism at Ephesus: 'So Paul left them (ie, the Jews in the synagoguge). He took the disciples with him and had discussions daily in the lecture hall of Tyrannus. This went on for two years, so that all the Jews and Greeks who lived in the province of Asia heard the word of the Lord' (Acts 19:9). Indeed, at one stage I was so convinced that the 'lecture' approach was the ideal that I encouraged the church to rent a neutral building (as distinct from the church) where we could put on a series of lectures on the Christian faith. Interestingly, our lecture series proved an utter disaster: hardly anybody came, and nobody was converted!

I now question the wisdom of separating evangelism from worship. Certainly, at the level of the local church the two belong together. It may be that in a university setting the lecture approach can be justified: I do, for instance, remember a very successful mission to Cambridge University led by the Anglican evangelist Michael Green, where the lecture approach was adopted. However, this should not be the norm. In saying this, I recognise the need — at every level of society — for people to be persuaded of the truth as it is in Jesus. The mind needs to be taken seriously. Interestingly, Luke makes it clear that Paul was often in the business of seeking to 'persuade' people of the truth of the Gospel: eg, 'Every Sabbath he reasoned in the synagogue, trying to persuade Jews and Greeks' (Acts 18:4); 'Paul entered the synagogue and spoke boldly therefore for three months, arguing persuasively about the Kingdom of God' (Acts 19:8; see also 19:26; 26:28; 28:23). Paul himself wrote to the church at Corinth: 'We try to persuade men' (2 Cor 5:11). But there is more to winning people to Christ than just appealing to their minds. People cannot simply be argued into the kingdom. Hearts need to be touched — and hearts are often touched not by what is heard, but by what is seen. It is in this context that church growth exponents have often talked of 3-P evangelism: before the Gospel can be proclaimed, and people persuaded of its truth, Christ has to be seen to be present in his people. It is such 'presence' which proves to be the sounding-board for the Gospel.

How is all this relevant to worship? In the fact that Christ can be seen to be present in his people, not only in the kind of lives they lead, but also in the worship they offer. The worship itself can be a sounding-board for the Gospel. Worship can prove to be winsome.

Worship that reveals Christ

Worship, where it is truly winsome, can prove to be effective in the service of the Gospel. Worship can, in fact, reveal Christ. This understanding of the relationship between worship and evangelism (sometimes referred to as 'celebration evangelism') was popularised in particular by the former Anglican evangelist, David Watson. For David Watson preferred not to preach at 'crusades', but at 'festivals'. His missions were always conducted within the context of praise. Here the worship was not always meaningful to the outsider, and yet nonetheless it proved to be exceedingly winsome.

David Watson expounded his approach in the following manner:

> Clearly it would be wrong to *use* worship as *a tool* for evangelism. True worship must always be first and foremost God-ward in its direction, even though the expression of worship, certainly in terms of serving and giving, may bring much blessing to other people. But when we are taken up with worship, and when we are unashamed of the fact that we are in love with God and in love with one another, that can be very powerful indeed. The world today is starved of love, suffocated with words, bereft of joy, and lacking in peace. Therefore 'a praising community preaches to answer questions raised by its praise'. So often, today, evangelism is crippled by the prevailing apathy. Comparatively few people are asking serious questions about God, partly because there is little or nothing which they see or hear to awake them to any sense of his reality. But when Christians are

to be found really worshipping God, loving him, serving him, excited with him, and when their worship makes them into a caring community of love, then questions will certainly be asked, leading to excellent opportunities for sharing the good news of Christ.[58]

I confess that I was greatly influenced by this approach. Guest services ceased to be the cerebral affairs they once were. Time was given to the worship of God. There is little doubt that the resulting worship proved impressive to the average pagan, whose experience of Christian worship was often limited to very dry and formal services elsewhere. I have little doubt that such worship did indeed prove to be a spring-board for the Gospel.

I often like to justify this approach to worship with a quotation from 1 Corinthians 14:25, where Paul writes that an unbeliever, as a result of experiencing Christian worship, 'will fall down and worship God, exclaiming, "God is really among you"'. However, the parallel is not quite exact, for in the situation Paul refers to the unbeliever is spoken to through a word of prophecy. This verse is primarily an argument for good preaching. Nonetheless, there seems to be no good reason why the verse cannot be applied to worship too.

The evening service and the unbeliever

Every worship service we lead should be winsome and thereby attractive to the outsider. Yet having recognised that fact, there is no doubt that some services are more appropriate for unbelievers than for others. My own experience, for instance, is that communion services tend to be inappropriate for unbelievers to attend. Indeed, I have known some churchgoing unbelievers to avoid those Sundays when we had morning communion — it made them feel uncomfortable, for they realised that they were not truly part of what was happening. In this respect my experience is directly contrary to that of David Watson, who wrote: 'Quite often during a communion service ..., when both service and sermon were directed almost exclusively to the convinced believer, I have seen men and women brought to faith in Christ, largely through the praise of God's people.'[59] Even David Watson, however, recognised that this is not quite the norm!

What services are more appropriate to the unbeliever? In some circles the morning service has been for the 'saints', and the evening service for the 'sinners'. This was, for instance, exemplified among the Christian Brethren, where the morning service centered around 'the breaking of bread', while the evening service took the form of a 'Gospel Service'. Such a pattern influenced many a Baptist church, where the morning service majored on teaching, and the evening service on evangelism. However, church life can never be as clear cut as this: sinners are to be found at both services. Certainly with the advent of morning Sunday School thirty years ago, together with the dropping off of attendance at the evening service, in many churches more 'sinners' are found at the morning service rather than in the evening.

One might therefore argue that today we should reverse the order: the needs of unbelievers should be uppermost in the morning service, while the needs of believers should be uppermost in the evening. Clearly there is no reason in principle why this should not happen. True, there would be difficulties for Christian families — husbands and wives would have to take it in turns to attend services, unless we followed the example of many American churches in providing nursery care during evening services. But if the Gospel is best furthered this way, then such difficulties should be relatively unimportant: after all, the church is, as William Temple used to say, the only society that exists for the sake of its non-members. Indeed, from within the context of Anglicanism, where the growth both of Parish

Communion and of Family Services has tended to push out the traditional sermon, David Kennedy and David Mann (*Sunday Evening Worship* p. 10), follow the lead of Colin Buchanan in *Patterns of Sunday Worship*, arguing that the evening service provides the best opportunities for teaching.

On the other hand, there is little doubt that evening services do still offer special opportunities for evangelism. Those without families — and such people form the majority of the population — in a British context still enjoy the traditional 'lie-in' on a Sunday morning. For such people an invitation to an evening service can be much more attractive than a similar invitation to a morning service. Furthermore, Sunday evening services do not normally suffer from the constraints of time in the same way as the morning services, which tend to have to be over within the hour for the sake of the children. However, if the evening service is to be geared — at least on occasion — for the unbeliever, then serious thought needs to be given to revising the timing of the average evening service. Why a 6.30 pm service? Nothing can be worse for the digestive system. 7 pm is much preferable — and 8 pm even more so. Maybe churches need to guided by the local bingo hall, which tends to be much more sensitive to people's needs. Let the needs of others — and not past church traditions — guide us in our planning for the unbeliever.

PART 2

CELEBRATING THE FESTIVALS

10

Celebrating Advent
— He comes!

Traditionally, the season of Advent marks the four weeks before Christmas. In these weeks the church prepares itself to celebrate the coming of Christ as a babe in a manger, and also looks forward to his coming again in glory.

In 1967 the Joint Liturgical Group produced their report *The Calendar and Lectionary*, in which they suggested a major re-ordering of this season before Christmas. They extended the Advent season to the nine Sundays before Christmas, and proposed that as part of the church's Advent preparation the first five of these Sundays (ie, the 'extra' five) should cover the themes of the creation, the fall, the election of God's people (Abraham), the promise of redemption (Moses), and the remnant. Interestingly, the Anglican *Alternative Service Book* also took up this suggestion.

However, much as a nine-week Advent season might commend itself to some liturgicists, it would be true to say that for the average church — and certainly the average Free Church — such a season would be five Sundays too long. The fact is that many churches have yet to begin to celebrate Advent at all. Realism would therefore indicate that it would be wise to go for the traditional four-week Advent season, and make the most of what that has to offer.

The *Alternative Service Book* lists the traditional focus of the four Advent Sundays as follows:

Advent 1 The Advent Hope
Advent 2 The Word of God in the Old Testament
Advent 3 The Forerunner
Advent 4 The Annunciation

With these four traditional themes in mind, I propose that we adopt the following nomenclature for these four special Sundays:

Advent 1 Advent Sunday
Advent 2 Bible Sunday
Advent 3 Ministry Sunday
Advent 4 Christmas Sunday

Let me clarify by elaborating on these four Advent Sundays.

Advent Sunday

Although Latin has now become a rarified subject, with the result that relatively few people can appreciate that the word 'Advent' comes from the Latin verb *advenio* (meaning, 'I draw near'), there still seems to be no viable alternative to the traditional title 'Advent Sunday'. Certainly 'Eschaton Sunday' is no improvement!

Advent Sunday is the Sunday in the church year when God's people focus on the Second Coming of Christ. Christ is coming again! In so far as this is a neglected theme in many a church, it is good to preach on this central tenet of the faith. Particularly for those churches who do not normally recite the creeds as part of their Sunday worship, it is good to be reminded of the truth that 'He will come again in glory to judge the living and the dead, and his kingdom will have no end' (Nicene Creed).

But there is more to Advent Sunday than preaching. Advent Sunday is also the day when the church begins to sing its way through the the Advent section of the hymn-book. Indeed, some churches organise special Advent carol services, inspired perhaps in part by the Advent services of the two Cambridge colleges, St John's and King's. These services take the form of a mixture of Advent carols and Advent readings. In *Carols for Choirs 2*, for instance, the suggested readings are: Isaiah 40:1–8; Jeremiah 23:5–6; Zechariah 9:9–16; Haggai 2:6–9; Isaiah 35:1–6; Romans 8:29–39; and Mark 1:1–15. (See also Michael Perham, *Liturgy Pastoral and Parochial*, p. 153). A church might not want to arrange such a service every year, but occasionally it would prove to be attractive. If one does go ahead marking Advent in such a way, it might be wise to describe the service in terms of 'Words and Music for Advent', for as Michael Perham helpfully points out, the term 'Advent carol service' can mislead people into expecting something more attuned to Christmas than is actually the case — for the heart of such a service lies not so much in the carols as in the Scriptures.[60]

Another way of celebrating Advent Sunday is to arrange a baptismal service on that day. *Praise God* commends this practice: 'The first Sunday in Advent, with its eschatological emphasis, provides a good opportunity for a baptismal service, the baptized being brought into the community of hope that awaits the coming of Christ.' Ephesians 2:12–13 could be a good text for such an occasion: 'Remember that at that time you were separate from Christ, without hope and without God in the world. But now in Christ Jesus you who once were far away have been brought near through the blood of Christ.'

Bible Sunday

The origin for Bible Sunday, popularised by the Bible Society in particular, is to be found in the Anglican collect for the day:

> Blessed Lord, who caused all holy Scriptures to be written for our learning: help us so to hear them, to read, mark, learn and inwardly digest them that, through patience, and the comfort of your holy word, we may embrace and for ever hold fast the hope

of everlasting life, which you have given us in our Saviour Jesus Christ.'

This is a good day for preaching on the word of God. However, perhaps even more importantly, this is a good day for encouraging people to read the Scriptures in a regular and systematic fashion. Wise pastors will not only make the most of the opportunity to press the need for personal Bible reading, they will also ensure that copies of Bible reading notes are available for people either to buy or order. There is a lot to be said for the church bookstall having a wide selection of Bibles and Bible handbooks for sale — many Christian bookshops will co-operate and offer books on a sale or return basis. God's people need to be a reading people — a people who read, above all, God's word.

Ministry Sunday

Advent 3 became associated with the 'ministry' because of the preparation for ordinations, which used to take place on Advent 4. The readings for the day in the *Alternative Service Book* are most appropriate:

Year 1 — Isaiah 40:1–11; 1 Corinthians 4:1–5; John 1:19–28.
Year 2 — Malachi 3:1–5; Philippians 4:4–9; Matthew 11:2–15.

Clearly, the emphasis here is on the Forerunner — John the Baptist. Whether or not the solo ministry of John the Baptist provides a good model for today's ordained ministry is no doubt debatable! The day does, however, provide an 'excuse' — or should I say 'reminder' — for churches to remember those pastors whom they have set aside for ministry. Interestingly, *Prayers for Today's Church*, under the heading of 'Third Sunday in Advent', has prayers not just 'for the Ministry' and 'those called to the Ministry', but also prayers for 'Theological Colleges' and for 'Retired Clergy'. Here is a mine to quarry! Further fuel for prayer may be gained by contacting former members whom the church at one time or another had sent out into pastoral ministry. It always amazes me how churches will keep in touch with those whom they have sent out into missionary service overseas, but then forget those whom they have sent out into service at home. Ministry Sunday, however, gives an opportunity to write or phone past members — and, indeed, even past pastors of the church — to find out their news and then pray for them all the more intelligently.

Along with praying goes preaching. Preaching should reflect the fact that not only are some called to special ministries of leadership and pastoral care, but also that all God's people are called to ministry of one kind or another. Ministry Sunday provides a welcome platform for preaching on every-member ministry.

Christmas Sunday

Strictly speaking, the Sunday after Christmas should bear this name. For it is not until Christmas Day itself that the Christmas season actually begins. Hence, in the more liturgically correct churches, Christmas carols are not sung until the clock has struck midnight on Christmas Eve. However, just as the High Street begins to celebrate Christmas from the autumn half-term onwards, so too do the vast majority of churches begin to celebrate Christmas before the 25th. The Sunday before Christmas — Christmas Sunday — is the day when most carol services are held.

Although carol services are sometimes held on the morning of 'Christmas Sunday', in my experience the best-attended carol services are always held in the evening. It is then that candles can be lit and the 'magic' of candlelight appreciated. 'Carols by candlelight' are a great attraction to the outsider. There is therefore everything to be said for unashamedly appealing to people's sentimentality by organising such services. Yes, 'services' — in the plural. With a certain amount of effort, it is possible to run at least two — if not three — services on a Christmas Sunday evening, with a packed church to boot.

One possibility is to stage a five o'clock service (when it is already dark) geared to the needs of young families, and a seven o'clock service for everybody else. It is best to limit the five o' clock service to forty-five minutes. It should include plenty of action for the children — whether allowing them to trot around the church singing 'Little Donkey', or building a manger alongside the pulpit. It should also include some traditional carols and readings. To keep people's attention during the readings, it can be helpful to dramatise the story or show slides of the nativity while the Scriptures are being read. The seven o'clock service can be a more sophisticated affair. Along with traditional carols (and it is the traditional carols that the average outsider expects) there can be newer songs; and along with the traditional readings there can be drama and dance. In both services there should be an evangelistic spot. This needn't be a full-blown sermon, but simply five minutes when children are present, and ten minutes at the later service. It should be just enough to make the real meaning of Christmas plain to all: the Word was made flesh, God has come to us, has become one of us.

To sustain interest from one year to another, it is vital that each year has a different theme. The Christmas message can be packaged in many and various ways. Why not turn the front of the church into a television studio and interview Mary in her old age? Mary remembers ... the visit of the angel Gabriel (Lk 1:26–35); the journey to Bethlehem and the birth of her son (Lk 2:1–15); the visit of the shepherds (Lk 2:8–20); the wise men (Mt 2:1–12); the old man who said that her son was a light for the world (Lk 2:22–32). Alternatively, the theme of God's promise can be developed. God promised Abraham that all nations would be blessed through his descendants (Gen 22:15–18); God promised Israel that his glory would be seen in them (Is 60:1–7); God promised Mary that she would bear a son (Lk 1:26–34); God promised Joseph that Mary's Son would be the Saviour of his people (Mt 1:18–25); God promised the shepherds that they would find a Saviour (Lk 2:8–18); God promised that all who accept the Christ will be his children (Jn 1:1–13).

Other possible themes for carol services include:

- *Promise and Fulfilment* (Is 9:2–3, 7; Lk 2:26–38; Mic 5:2–3; Lk 2:1–7; Is 11:1–9; Lk 2:8–16; Is 60:1–7; Mt 2:1–12).
- *Christ the Light of the World* (Call to worship: Jn 1:4–5; the prophet sees the coming Messiah as a great light: Is 9:2–9; Zechariah foresees a day to lighten our darkness: Lk 1:67–79; the light shines in the darkness: Lk 2:1–7; the shepherds see the light of God's glory: Lk 2:1–7; Simeon rejoices to see God's light in a babe: Lk 2:25–33; the wise men bring their tribute to Jesus, the Light of the world: Mt 2:12).
- *Christ the King* (Look, your king is coming: Zech 9:9; the promise of a king: Is 9:2, 6, 7; Mic 5:2; Mary is told she will bear a son who will be king: Lk 1:26–38; Angels proclaim the Lordship of the new baby: Lk 2:8–16; wise men seek Jesus the king: Mt 2:1–12; Jesus the King of creation: Col 1:15–20).
- *God's Gift Of Love* (Call to worship: 2 Cor 9:15; the gift is promised: Is 7:14; 9:2, 6, 7; Mary is to bear the gift: Lk 1:26–38; Angels announce the gift: Lk 2:8–14; the shepherds find the gift: Lk 2:15–19; the wise men bring their gifts: Mt 2:1–11; the gift is threatened: Mt 2:13–18; receive the gift: Jn 3:16–21).

Clearly, many of the same readings keep on recurring. Variety, however, is to be found in the way in which the readings are introduced and arranged, and the way in which carols are sensitively combined with the readings. As a diamond may be turned in the light, allowing various facets of the stone to shine and sparkle in differing ways, so using differing approaches we seek to approach the Christmas story and see fresh facets of its truth.

Celebrating Advent with candles

Candles should not just be limited to Christmas Sunday itself. Advent candles should be a feature of the whole season. Here I have in mind the four red Advent candles traditionally placed around a green advent wreath, with perhaps a white candle in the middle ready to be lit on Christmas Day. On each Advent Sunday a candle may be lit. The children will love it. And not just the children. The whole church will begin to share in the excitement of preparing to celebrate the coming of the Christ-child.

No doubt to the true Puritan this custom of lighting Advent candles sounds dreadfully papist. But to do away with candles — at Advent at least — is to run the danger of throwing out the baby with the bathwater. Certainly, when symbols are combined with the reading of God's word, a powerful force is unleashed.

One way of combining the lighting of the candles with the reading of God's word is to ask a different family to share in a 'candlelighting ceremony' which links with an appropriate reading for the day. For instance, the following readings may be used for the four Sundays of Advent — they presuppose two 'voices', one of which may be a child, the other an adult (the rest of the family can assist with the lighting of the candles).

Advent 1

Voice 1: We light this first Advent candle to remind us of the Advent hope — Jesus is coming again!

Voice 2: The night is nearly over, the day is almost here. So let us put aside the deeds of darkness, and put on the armour of light (Rom 13:12).

Advent 2

Voice 1: We light these two Advent candles to remind us of God's gift the Bible — the Bible points us to Jesus, the Light of the world.

Voice 2: The Apostle Peter writes: 'You will do well to pay attention to the word of the prophets, as to a light shining in a dark place, until the day dawns and the morning star rises in your hearts' (2 Pet 1:19).

Advent 3

Voice 1: We light these three Advent candles to remind us of John the Baptist and of all God's messengers who prepare the way for the Saviour's coming.

Voice 2: There came a man who was sent from God; his name was John. He came as a witness to testify concerning that light, so that through him all men might believe (Jn 1:6–7).

Advent 4

Voice 1: We light these four Advent candles to remind us of our calling to reflect the light of Jesus in this dark world.

Voice 2: Jesus said: 'You are the light of the world. . . . Let your light shine before men, that they may see your good deeds and praise your Father in heaven' (Mt 5:14–16).

Christmas Day

Voice 1: We light this Christmas candle to remind us that Jesus is the Light of the world.

Voice 2: To us a child is born, to us a son is given. . . . Glory to God in the highest, and on earth peace to men on whom his favour rests (Is 9:6; Lk 2:14).

Preaching through Advent

Most congregations find it helpful if there is a theme running through the Advent preaching. At times the preaching will reflect the particular Sunday itself, and at other times it will be part of a series which is leading up to Christmas in a more general way.

Such series may centre around Bethlehem. For example:
Bethlehem — The Grave of Rachael (Gen 35:16–20; Mt 2:16–18).
Bethlehem — The Well of Sacrifice (2 Sam 23:13–17).
Bethlehem — The Home of Ruth (Ruth 1:1–19a).
Bethlehem — the City of David (Lk 2:10–11).

Or they may focus on the theme of light. For example:
Light at the end of the tunnel (Mk 13).
Light from God's word (2 Pet 1:19).
Witnessing to the Light (Jn 1:5–7; 3:25–30).
Obedience to the Light (Lk 1:38)

Again, with the emphases of the various Advent Sundays in mind, one may preach on the Kingdom of God:
The Coming of the Kingdom (Mt 6:10).
The Growth of the Kingdom (Mt 13:31–35).
The Grace of the Kingdom (Mt 20:1–16).
The Crisis of the Kingdom (Mt 21:33–43).

Other possibilities include focussing on personalities (eg, Zechariah, Mary, Joseph, Simeon), or on the songs of the nativity (eg, The Benedictus, the Magnificat, the Gloria). The possibilities are many and varied, provided one is prepared to use one's mind creatively.

Celebrating Christmas
— the Lord has come!

Christmas is a time for celebration: 'A Saviour has been born ... Christ the Lord' (Lk 2:11). Yet strangely some churches — not least many Free Churches — have failed to celebrate the day itself. The Christmas Eve service, so popular in Roman Catholic and Anglican churches, is far from being the norm in the Free Churches, in Britain at least. Likewise the Christmas Day service is not always the packed occasion it might be. In some areas, for instance, Christmas Morning is an occasion for a 'united' service — as if otherwise the individual churches would find it difficult on their own to muster a decent congregation. Fortunately things are changing, and Christmas Day is beginning to get the recognition it deserves. Nonetheless, in most churches the best congregations are still found on the Sunday before Christmas rather than Christmas Day itself. I hope this chapter will encourage the trend towards making the most of Christmas itself.

Christmas Eve

Christmas Eve services are traditionally eucharistic in nature. And why not? What better way is there to welcome in Christmas Day than to remember the coming of the Lord Jesus around the Communion Table. 'The Son of Man came not to be served, but to serve and to give his life as a ransom

135

for many' (Mk 10:45). The Babe of Bethlehem was born to be the Christ of Calvary. God's people have indeed much to celebrate. A quiet candlelit celebration of the Lord's Supper on Christmas Eve can be an immensely moving experience. There is no better way of putting Christmas in its true perspective than to eat bread and drink wine and in this way focus one's mind upon God's greatest gift.

However, as at any other Communion service, the word needs to accompany the sacrament. On Christmas Eve in particular, this word needs to be evangelistic in nature. For experience shows that Christmas Eve is when those on the church fringe — and often beyond the fringe — attend church. John 3:16 is very much the heart of the Gospel message.

The Christmas Eve service therefore presents a tension: on the one hand, it is an occasion for God's people to celebrate the faith; on the other hand, it is an occasion for the faith to be proclaimed. Churches often succumb to the temptation of resolving the tension by doing the one to the exclusion of the other. Ideally both should be attempted.

At what time should such a service be held? Although 'Midnight Mass' is the norm in many churches, it is not unknown to hold the service much earlier. Indeed, in some Continental countries the service can even be in the late afternoon. My own personal preference is to begin the service at 11.15 pm and end at 12.05 am. On the one hand I see no reason to wait until midnight before eating bread and drinking wine; on the other hand I recognise the desire of many to welcome in Christmas Day. Too late a service will mean that fewer people turn up to the Christmas Morning service!

What kind of 'order' would be appropriate for such a service? The following is a specimen order of service:

Call to worship   John 1:14 ('The Word became flesh')

HYMN	All my heart this night rejoices
Prayers praise and confession	
Scriptures	Eg, Isaiah 9:2, 6f; Lk 2:1–20
HYMN	It came upon the midnight clear
Address	(Ten minutes maximum!)
Prayer of response	
HYMN	See him a-lying on a bed of straw
Welcome and Invitation to the Table	
Scriptures	Eg, John 3:16
Words of institution	
Prayer of thanksgiving	
Bread and wine	
Prayers and songs of praise	(eg, Jesus name above all names; Emmanuel, Emmanuel)
Prayer of dedication	
Christmas greeting	'A Happy Christmas!'
HYMN	O come all you faithful
The Grace	

A number of comments need to be made on this specimen order.

1) It is important to choose *a good number of traditional carols* on such an occasion. People want to sing the carols they have known and loved. This does not rule out modern songs altogether — but they need to be limited. Furthermore, they need to be apposite. Hence the simple 'Jesus' songs for singing after receiving the bread and wine.

2) *The Scripture readings need to be appropriate* to the occasion. Isaiah 9, with its mention of 'the people who have walked in darkness have seen a great light', and also Luke 2, with its account of the midnight angelic chorus, are both very suitable.

3) *Christmas Eve is not the best occasion for a full-blooded sermon*. People have come to celebrate, not listen to a twenty-five minute address. If the sermon goes on this long, people will probably switch off. Far better a ten-minute evangelistic address. But let its brevity not be an excuse for minimal preparation. It takes time to produce a well-honed address, however short it is.

4) Precisely because a good number of non-Christians are likely to be present, it is important that *the invitation to the Table be clearly worded*. The Lord's Table is for the Lord's people. This does not mean that those who are not the Lord's are not to feel welcome — far from it, they should be told how delighted the church is to have visitors on this special occasion. However, the bread and wine are for those who have committed their lives to the Lord who loved them and gave himself for them. Needless to say, careful preparation is needed in the form of words that are used.

5) *Instead of the 'Peace', let the congregation wish one another a Happy Christmas*. Where the service starts at 11.15 pm, there is much to be said for the pastor/worship leader keeping a careful eye on the time, so that as Christmas Day begins one can declare, 'Midnight has struck! It is Christmas Day! A Happy Christmas to you all! Let's get up out of our seats and greet one another in a seasonal way!'

6) *The service climaxes with 'O come all you faithful'*. It may seem needless to stress that this is above all a carol for Christmas Day. Yet strangely enough there are churches which two or three weeks before Christmas happily sing, 'Yea, Lord, we greet Thee/Born this happy morning'! Clearly, for some a good deal of reinterpretation is necessary!

Christmas Day

Just as for most people Christmas Day is *the* family occasion, so too for many people Christmas Day is *the* family occasion in the church. This is the day when the whole family wants to go to church and celebrate the birth of Christ the Lord. If, however, the Christmas Day Morning Service is to be for all the family, then two things need to be remembered:

First, the service should be relatively short. With a turkey in the oven and all the other trimmings to think about, no mother will want to be away from home for too long. But if, for example, the service lasts for an hour and a half — which in turn means that the family may well be away from home for well over two hours — some will want to stay at home to look after the Christmas dinner. It is surely far better therefore to limit the service to forty-five minutes, and in this way ensure the presence of the whole family. Forty-five minutes may not sound long, but good preparation combined with discipline on the day can result in quite a full service being put together.

Secondly, if the Christmas Day service is for the whole family, then it is important that there is something for every member of the family. This means that there is something for the children, but something for adults too. The right blend is not always easy to achieve. On the one hand it is very easy for the service to become a children's service, on the other hand, it is very easy for the service to lose the children's attention. A fast-moving order of service — with plenty of visuals — is required. The sermon needs to be in the region of ten to fifteen minutes — though geared for the adults, it should be intelligible to an eleven-year-old, and should be illustrated with good overheads.

With these two needs in mind, I offer a specimen order for a Christmas Morning Service, lasting forty-five minutes, in which all ages are present.

Lighting of Christmas Candle
HYMN: Christians awake, salute the
                                   happy morn
Prayers of praise
  and confession

Welcome to visitors	(Who has come the farthest?)
Welcome to children	(Who was awake the earliest?)
It's Christmas-present time	the children show their presents!
HYMN:	God rest you merry gentlemen
It's Christmas in Africa too!	Third World spot
Offering for Christian Aid/ Tear Fund	
Musical item	
Scriptures	
HYMN:	Good Christian men rejoice and sing
Address	[fifteen minutes maximum!]
Prayer of response	
HYMN:	O come all you faithful
Benediction	

12

Celebrating the Turning of the Year
— ring out the old, ring in the new!

The word 'January' comes from the Latin *Janus*, the name of an ancient Roman deity. Primarily a god of gates and doors, Janus was famous for having two faces looking in opposite directions, in this way probably symbolising the two faces of a door. The month named after Janus likewise has two faces — facing the end of one year, and the beginning of another. These two moments in time, within a Christian context, call for celebration. They are natural moments for God's people to look both backwards and forwards and celebrate the faithfulness of God.

The last Sunday of the year

The Sunday after Christmas is often a difficult Sunday. What on earth is one to preach on? No doubt the more liturgically-minded would reply 'Christmas!' But by that Sunday most people are 'fed up' with Christmas. Having gorged themselves on turkey and stuffed themselves on Christmas pudding, they want a change of diet. Yet to announce a new series on Paul's Letter to the Romans doesn't seem quite right either.

So what then? One solution I have found helpful is to use the last Sunday evening service of the year as an occasion for thanksgiving. Members of the congregation can be invited to share testimonies of God's goodness to them over the past

141

twelve months. Indeed, the whole service can be entitled 'Thank God for 19..'.

Needless to say, such a service demands a good deal of preparation. It cannot be left to Christmas week itself! It takes time, for instance, to discover who will not have gone away for Christmas. It also takes time to ensure that there is a balance to the testimonies. But the time and effort taken can be so worthwhile. One person might speak of the joy of coming to know the Lord; another of God's encouragement while away at university; a third perhaps of her gratitude to God for the gift of a child; while yet another might speak of the strength received to cope with bereavement. Inevitably such a service holds great human interest. But even more importantly, it testifies to the grace of God in all life's situations.

With thanksgiving as the theme, how might such an order look?

Call to worship	
HYMN:	Now thank we all our God
Prayer	— thanking God for all the blessings of the past
	— seeking forgiveness for the times when we magnified our troubles and overlooked God's goodness
Psalm 103	Bless the Lord, O my soul.
Songs of praise and thanksgiving	eg, I will enter his gates with thanksgiving in my heart
	Rejoice in the Lord always
	I will sing, I will sing a song unto the Lord
Offering	
Notices	for the New Year!
HYMN:	What a friend we have in Jesus
Testimony	eg, a recent convert
Testimony	eg, a Christian of longstanding

Song	Yesterday, today, for ever, Jesus is the same
Testimony	
Testimony	
HYMN	He lives, he lives, Christ Jesus lives today!
Testimonies galore:	each person to share with their neighbour 'in the pew' one good thing the Lord has done for them over the past year
Testimony	
Testimony	
Song	I will give thanks to Thee
Scriptures	
Address	(Ten minutes maximum)
Prayers	
HYMN	Great is thy faithfulness
The Grace	

A number of comments need to be made about the above order.

First, it may seem rather formal when in fact the service should have a relaxed feel to it. In a sense, the pastor or worship leader acts as a Master of Ceremonies as he or she introduces the various people who have been asked to share their testimony. What's more, let the introductions be introductions. Instead of saying, 'Now Bill Bloggs will say what God has done for him over the past twelve months,' say, 'Bill Bloggs is married to Sally, and works for the local fireservice. Last July we had the joy of seeing Bill baptised in this church. Bill is now going to share what God has done for him over the last twelve months.'

The way in which the testimonies are given should vary. Some may give their testimonies 'straight'; others might prefer to give it in an interview style; yet others might like to include as part of their testimony a poem they have written or a song they would like to sing. There is much to be said for each testimony being linked with a particular verse of Scripture. For inevitably testimonies are subjective, whereas there is a certain objectiveness about the word of God

The testimonies should be disciplined. A time limit of five minutes maximum should be imposed. Those giving testimonies should be encouraged to write out what they want to say. They may not necessarily read their script, but should nonetheless keep to the general outline.

In the above order, there is place for a 'corporate testimony' in which everybody is encouraged to share with one another God's goodness to them. This spot needs to be handled with sensitivity. Some people may be present who are so overwhelmed by their troubles that they find it difficult to see any light; alternatively, there may be people present who have yet to commit their lives to Christ. It may well be, therefore, that for some this time of sharing may simply prove to be an extended time of greeting one another. On the other hand, the general challenge to the congregation to be mindful of God's goodness to each one should certainly be present.

With six or so people involved in giving testimonies, there will be no time left for a full-blown sermon. Even so, it is still good to give a brief exposition of God's word. Appropriate passages could include Romans 8:28 ('We know that in all things God works for the good of those who love him'); Phillipians 1:3–11 ('I thank my God for your partnership in the Gospel'); 1 Thessalonians 5:16–18 ('Give thanks in all circumstances').

If my experience is anything to go by, such a service of testimony and thanksgiving can easily render what might have been a 'Low Sunday' into a 'High Sunday'. There is nothing more stimulating to one's faith than listening to fellow Christians tell of God's gracious action in their lives. To look back with thanksgiving is indeed to end the year on a high note.

The Watchnight Service

Watchnight services are Methodist in origin. Although now generally confined to New Year's Eve, Watchnight services were originally eighteenth-century equivalents of today's charismatic 'celebrations'. Thus, according to David Tripp:

> The watch-night began in spontaneous meetings held by enthusiastic Methodists in Kingswood (a mining area near Bristol), who often spent 'the greater part of the night in prayer, and praise, and thanksgiving'. Discovering these unofficial gatherings, probably in the early spring of 1742, John Wesley adopted and regularized the idea. ... Within a few months the watchnight had become a regular event at the main Methodist centres (Bristol, London, Newcastle), held from about 8.30 p.m. to about 12.30 a.m.on the Friday nearest the full moon, so that members walked safely home through moonlit streets. It was also held on public and Methodist fast-days, and especially on New Year's Eve'.[61]

Although Watchnight services are no longer held on the Fridays nearest the full moon, a good number of churches still retain the New Year's Eve Watchnight service. True, it has been somewhat watered down: the whole evening is no longer given over to praise and prayer! For the most part services do not begin until 11.15 pm, or even 11.30 pm.

Watchnight services are not so well attended as they were in earlier days, with the result that many churches have given up on them. However, there is much to commend holding this particular service: the turning of the year is a good time for looking backwards with thanksgiving, and for looking forwards with faith; it is a time, too, to remind oneself of the brevity of life and to dedicate the coming year to God.

How, then, might one encourage people to attend a watchnight service? In the first place, attendance might be encouraged by holding a church party earlier in the evening (starting at 8.30 pm as did the earlier Methodist services), which could then run into the watchnight service proper. At the end of the day, however, it will be the quality of the actual event which will either draw people or not. An imaginative service carefully prepared — as distinct from some songs thrown together with one or two devotional thoughts for good measure — can rival anything that might be on the 'box'. Once a good tradition has established itself, there is less need for a church party to act as a draw.

The first Sunday of the year

The first Sunday of the year is a time for looking forwards. It is the Sunday when many pastors encourage their people to renew their faith in the God who goes ahead. It is very much an 'upbeat' Sunday. It's an occasion for giving the church a 'motto' for the year — whether printed on a card or simply enshrined within a sermon.

New Year is also a time for making New Year's resolutions. It's a very natural time for people to seek to turn over a new leaf and start afresh in their lives. Alas, those New Year's resolutions are generally shortlived. If we rely on our own strength, we fail. Far better to seek the Lord's strength. Hence many churches use the first communion service of the year as a time when God's people are encouraged to rededicate their lives to the Lord and seek his enabling power to live more consistent Christian lives.

Methodists have traditionally formalised such a service of rededication within the context of a 'covenant service', first instituted by John Wesley. Here the congregation renews its covenant with the Lord in the following time-honoured words: 'I am no longer my own, but thine. Put me to what thou wilt, rank me with whom thou wilt; put me to doing, put me to suffering; let me be employed for thee or laid aside for thee, exalted for thee or brought low for thee.'

The tradition of covenant renewal is, of course, not

exclusively Methodist. It has been very much a feature of Baptist life too. The Baptist church meeting in Chester Street, Wrexham (the church within which my wife was brought up), has a long tradition of reading together on the first Sunday of the year its church covenant of 1773:

'We, the members of the Baptist Independent Church in Wrexham professing the belief of the doctrine of free, sovereign, and efficacious grace, do acknowledge the riches of that grace of God in providing a Saviour for us wretched sinners, even the Lord Jesus Christ: his goodness in sending the Gospel to us, at the ends of the earth; giving us some experience of the power of that Gospel in our souls (through the sacred operations of his Holy Spirit), humbling, comforting, charging, renewing us, calling us to be a part of his church in this world; and fixing a pastor over us; and we do now in the name and in the fear of God, give up ourselves to the Lord and to one another by the will of God; desiring to walk together in church fellowship according to the rules of the Gospel, that is to say — conscientiously to sanctify the Lord's Day; to attend on the public preaching of the Word and the administration of the ordinances of Christ, church meetings and meetings of prayer, unless some unavoidable hindrance prevent; to walk with and watch over one another in love; endeavouring in the strength of divine grace to maintain the unity of the Spirit in the bond of peace, to keep up the life of religion in our own souls, the exercise of daily prayer in private and in our families (not forgetting, at such seasons, the peace and prosperity of Zion, and of our own church and pastor in particular); and to walk uprightly and circumspectly in our own families and before the world, that others may see our good works, and may glorify our Father who is in heaven. Amen!'

Although a covenant of this kind helps to make a church aware of its roots, it is perhaps questionable whether the language used still retains its original force. Better, perhaps, for churches to compose a covenant in contemporary language. Nonetheless this old covenant is helpful, in so far as it is a reminder that commitment to the Lord involves commitment to one another. It is this corporate aspect of the Baptist church covenants which distinguishes them from the covenant used in the traditional Methodist service. Needless to say, in a Baptist context at least, for a covenant to be meaningful, it must first be brought to a church meeting and the church given the opportunity to 'own' it, before it is actually used within a worship service.

One word of warning, however. Although it is good for a church to rededicate itself to the Lord and to one another, such opportunities can be overworked. Once or twice a year is fine. But if such opportunities are given not only at the beginning of the New Year, but also in September as the church starts up its work after the summer, at Easter to mark the renewal of baptismal vows, on Stewardship Sunday, and also at the Church Anniversary, then something of the solemnity of the occasion disappears!

A week of prayer

In many churches, January is the month for prayer. The Evangelical Alliance, for instance, normally calls churches to prayer in this period. Similarly, the World Council of Churches and its member bodies have their 'Week of Prayer for Church Unity'.

Without neglecting these special prayer emphases which tend to have the wider church in view, there is much to be said for local churches beginning the New Year by emphasising their dependence on the Lord within their own more localised spheres. One possibility is to cancel all normal church activities in the first full week of the New Year, and devote either an evening or a series of evenings to prayer. For instance, one evening could be devoted to prayer for the local community: church members could be briefed to share concerns for which they feel the church should be praying — maybe a centre for families under stress, or the teaching of Religious Studies in a neighbourhood school, or the local MP along with local councillors (how often are such people actually named in church?). Another evening could be devoted to church concerns: here leaders of church activities could be asked to report on the encouragements and difficulties they are facing. A third evening could focus on mission, at home and abroad: the church's missionary secretary could, for instance, be asked to have ready news of the church's missionaries or link-missionaries. With imaginative preparation, such evenings for prayer can prove most stimulating and informative, and thus turn out to be quite memorable occasions. But, let me emphasise, at the end of the day everything depends on the level of preparation. Good prayer meetings do not normally just hap en.

Epiphany

January 6th is the day in the church's year when the 'manifestation' of God to the world in Jesus Christ is traditionally celebrated. In the Eastern church this was related both to the birth and baptism of Jesus. In the Western church it became the day for celebrating the visit of the wise men to Jesus. In recent liturgical revisions, however, the West has built the theme of the baptism of Jesus into its Epiphany celebrations. Thus in the Anglican *Alternative Service Book*, the baptism of Jesus is the theme for the First Sunday after Epiphany. In the light of these changes, the Baptist manual *Praise God*, (p. 14) comments: 'Epiphany provides us with an opportunity of expounding the meaning of baptism in the context of the continuing mission of the church in the world'.

Epiphany probably doesn't feature very strongly in the life of most Free Churches. Nonetheless, there might be some mileage in its occasional celebration, especially when linked to a service of believers' baptism. The baptismal service could actually turn into a commissioning service, as hands are laid on the newly baptised and prayer is made that they be filled afresh with God's Spirit with a view to sharing with others the Good News of Jesus. In the words of the Indian Bishop, Bishop Azariah: 'I am a baptised Christian. Woe unto me if I preach not the Gospel!'

13

Celebrating Lent and Holy Week
— *a season of preparation*

Preparing to celebrate

The English word 'Lent' means 'Spring'. But Lent is not primarily a spring festival, but rather a pre-Easter period of spiritual discipline. Strictly speaking, it is incorrect to speak of 'celebrating' Lent, for Lent does not celebrate anything — rather it is a season of preparation for celebrating the death and resurrection of Jesus. The observance of Lent was first undertaken by candidates for baptism on Easter Day — the period of their instruction being spread over six weeks. Today, however, Lent has become the time when Christians in general are invited to prepare themselves to celebrate the events of Good Friday and Easter Day.

Lent has also become associated with the forty days Jesus spent in the wilderness following his baptism. In the words of *Praise God* (p. 17): 'Just what thoughts filled his mind we can never know, for it is likely that besides matters of personal obedience Jesus also wrestled over the nature of God's mission to the world and the future of the nation. Lent therefore carries with it a call to corporate as well as personal repentance. It is a time for self-examination and an opportunity to deepen the devotional life of both the individual Christian and the fellowship of the church as well as an occasion to assess the church's responsibility to the world.' An interesting suggestion!

From a Free Church perspective, Lent does not normally

have much if any significance in the worship life of the church. The kind of services embodied in the General Synod publication *Lent, Holy Week, Easter* are foreign to free churchmen. The penitential litanies of Ash Wednesday just do not feature. Indeed, if anything, Lent is associated with ecumenical Bible study groups — which are fine for those churches which do not normally run house groups, but for those who do are often a veritable form of penance, complicating, as they do, the normal routine of church life!

From a preacher's perspective, Lent does offer an opportunity to preach on some of the Christian basics — either as an introductory course to the Christian faith with new Christians in mind (taking up the idea of Lent as being a period of preparation for baptism), or as a refresher course with the needs of the congregation in general in mind. One possibility would be to preach a special series of sermons on the life of Christ; alternatively one could preach on some of the Christian disciplines (eg, Bible-reading; prayer; worship; fellowship; evangelism; service).

Mothering Sunday/Mothers' Day

To a liturgical purist, Mothering Sunday just does not exist. There is no reference to it in such a standard work as *A New Dictionary of Liturgy and Worship*. Nonetheless it does exist: Mothering Sunday is in fact the third Sunday before Easter Sunday. Strictly speaking, it was the day when 'Mother Church' was remembered. It was the occasion when people working away from home returned to their families (bearing gifts of flowers and simnel cake) and thus to their home churches.

If this theme of Mother Church is pursued, then all sorts of ideas suggest themselves.

1) It can be a day when we invite back to the church all those who have been baptised as believers (or confirmed in their faith) over the past few years. Not only can this be an

opportunity to renew fellowship with those who have moved away, it can also be an opportunity to renew contact with those who still live in the district, but who for one reason or another have lapsed in their church attendance.

2) It can be a day when we invite back to the church all those who have brought their children for a service of dedication (or its equivalent) over the past few years. Again, this may well offer an opportunity to renew contact with those who have ceased to attend church. It also offers an opportunity to remind all parents of the responsibilities of Christian parenthood.

3) It can be a day when we celebrate the church's anniversary. Many a church is somewhat vague as to when it came into being. Mothering Sunday is as good a Sunday as any to celebrate our life together in Christ.

But there is a further aspect connected to Mothering Sunday. Whatever its origins, commerce — in the UK at least — dictates that we also celebrate it as Mothers' Day. In so far as there is nothing sacrosanct about Mothering Sunday, there is no reason why we should not go with the tide and celebrate it as Mothers' Day — especially if we can 'exploit' it for Christian purposes. Indeed, this is precisely what was done by a leaflet put out by the Christian Publicity Organisation:

> MUMS — you have been heavenly appointed! In God's wisdom he planned life in such a way as to make the role of 'Mum' irreplaceable. Through the years of growth from toddler to teenager it's Mum's influence which will most direct the development of the child. It is a heavy and serious responsibility. The message of this Mothers' Day is — Never underestimate the importance of 'Mum', God doesn't. And Mums, as you receive the support of family, friends and neighbours, don't forget your greatest supporter is Jesus Christ.

Mothers' Day is rightly a day to celebrate motherhood. There is so much for which most of us, at least, should be grateful. But in spite of the happy associations of Mothers' Day, there are dangers.

It can focus unduly on mothers with young children, with the result that mothers with children who have grown up and moved away can be forgotten. Even worse, the focus can be so much on mothers, that the childless can be made to feel either guilty or unfulfilled. One way to get round this danger is to ensure that posies of flowers are given by the children not just to their mothers, but to all the ladies in the church. Let every lady feel special!

It can focus on mothers to the detriment of fathers! This no doubt sounds an unneccesarily sexist comment, but in these days when single-parent families are becoming increasingly common, there are families where the parent caring for the children is the father. One way to get around this particular danger is ensuring that in the prayers such families are remembered.

Passion Sunday

Passion Sunday does not come high up on the liturgical calendar. Few people in the Free Churches are even aware that it is the second Sunday before Easter. Yet Passion Sunday affords an opportunity for us to remember the 'passion' ie, the suffering — of Jesus. In churches where there is no tradition of following the sufferings of our Lord during the week running up to Easter, there is always the danger of rushing from Palm Sunday to Easter Sunday without truly reflecting on the cross. Passion Sunday provides an opportunity to focus on the cross.

Palm Sunday

Palm Sunday is, of course, the day on which the church celebrates Christ's triumphal entry into Jerusalem. This is the day for a 'Jesus demo'. This is a day for declaring that 'our God reigns'!

Trevor Lloyd tells how 'in at least one English village the

congregation meet outside the village, coming in to church preceeded by a donkey, the crowd singing and carrying bamboo leaves for palms'.[62] Not all of us have access to a donkey — and even if we did, we might well question the wisdom of using it. For ultimately we are not in the business of re-enacting a past event, but commemorating a present reality. In the words of *Lent, Holy Week, Easter:* Palm Sunday 'is an act of praise to Christ the king who reigns and triumphs on the cross, and it expresses our own readiness to take up our cross and follow our crucified and risen Lord'.[63]

Donkeys smack of archaism. We must find ways of expressing in contemporary idiom the message of Palm Sunday. Marian E. Musselthwaite suggests a parade service beginning with the National Anthem. 'Beginning from reference to the National Anthem,' she writes, 'use question and answer to establish the nature of kingship, the qualities of a ruler and the reasons for calling God "King of kings"'.[64] But even such a suggestion is dated: young people — and not so young people — no longer appreciate singing the National Anthem, or at least not in church. Perhaps the best way forward is to hand one of the Palm Sunday services over to the young people — they often know best how to celebrate!

Holy Week

Holy Week — a term which I personally dislike, but which nonetheless is becoming increasingly normative — begins on Palm Sunday and ends on Easter Day. The Reformers largely abolished the observance of this particular week, but in this century in particular there has been a revival of interest in it, with the result that in some of the more liturgical churches every day is given special meaning and marked by a special service.

But the question arises: can the average church cope with a whole week of special services? Is it realistic to lay on services for every day of the week? Or is it more a matter of the pastor laying on a host of goodies from which people can pick and choose? If this last scenario is true, then the church presents to the world the most unappetising model of being a kind of spiritual cafeteria. Surely a wiser course is to limit the number of special services with a view to gaining the whole-hearted participation of the church at every service. Palm Sunday and Easter Day apart, the two great services would be Maundy Thursday and Good Friday. Interestingly, Michael Perham also argues for a limitation to Holy Week services in order that the four great days of Palm Sunday, Maundy Thursday, Good Friday and Easter Day receive absolute priority. He writes:

> To attend on only one or two of these days is like hearing some, but not all, the movements of a symphony. Pleasure there may be, but there cannot be real understanding, real entering in, without the experience of the whole. In order to help people to find time for these four great movements in the symphony, the diary of Holy Week should not be overloaded in other ways.[65]

Maundy Thursday

The term 'Maundy Thursday' is derived through the Old French word *mande* from the Latin *mandatum novum*, meaning a new commandment'. There is a reference back to John's account of the Upper Room, in which he records that the Lord gave his disciples 'a new commandment . . . to love one another' (Jn 13:34). In John 13 this commandment was given in the context of footwashing, with the result that originally Maundy Thursday services included the washing of feet. Although some churches have revived this particular custom of footwashing, it is questionable whether such a gesture has any meaning in our culture. More culturally relevant ways could be found to give depth to the Lord's command to love and serve one another. Indeed, one simple way of expressing love for one another is to pray for one another. Maundy Thursday could well be a day when, within the context of a communion service, opportunity is given for people to come forwards and ask for prayer.

Whatever, Maundy Thursday is certainly a natural occasion for celebrating the Lord's Supper. It commemorates the fact that it was on the night before he was betrayed that Jesus instituted this feast of remembrance. Furthermore, in so far as it is a midweek occasion, it lends itself to doing things differently from the Sunday norm. The very setting can be more informal: the Lord's Supper could, for instance, be celebrated in the round. Alternatively, it is possible to celebrate the Lord's Supper within the context of an 'Agape' meal — the love feast being a vivid reminder that our Lord broke bread and poured out wine within the context of a meal.

Good Friday

Good Friday lends itself to all kinds of possibilities, although in some areas things are complicated by the fact that it is a working day.

Within the Anglican tradition, Good Friday is often marked by a service of three hours' devotion, usually based on guided meditations on the seven words which Jesus spoke from the cross: 'Father, forgive them, for they do not know what they are doing' (Lk 23:34); 'Today you will be with me in paradise' (Lk 23:43); 'Here is your son. ... Here is your mother' (Jn 19:26–27); 'My God, my God, why have you forsaken me?' (Mt 27:45–46); 'I am thirsty' (Jn 19:28); 'It is finished' (Jn 19:30); 'Father, into your hands I commit my spirit' (Lk 23:46). In this connection the Baptist manual *Praise God* (p. 22) suggests that the service of three hours' devotion be combined with the service of 'tenebrae': *tenebrae*, a Latin word meaning shadows or dark hours, refers to the practice of gradually extingushing the lights (candles) during the course of the service. *Praise God*, for instance, envisages seven candles being lit before the service:

'At the end of each section of the service one of the candles is extinguished as the appropriate word is repeated. The service ends with the extingushing of the last candle immediately followed by the benediction'.

Clearly, there are other ways in which a congregation can be helped to meditate on the sufferings and death of our Lord. Thus Philip Gouldson has set out an order of service whereby a simple display of the objects of the cross is allowed to make an impact with the help of the narration of the incident with which they are associated. For example, a bottle of wine (Mt 27:34; Lk 23:12–26); a cross (Jn 19:17); a hammer and nails (Jn 19:18; Lk 23:17–28); an indictment (Jn 19:19); a robe (Jn 19:2; Lk 23:39-49); a crown of thorns (Jn 19:2); a sponge (Jn 19:29); a spear (Jn 19:34–35).[66] There are many possibilities for an imaginative approach.

Evangelism and Holy Week

Even if a church could cope with a whole week of special services — not just Maundy Thursday and Good Friday — would it be right? Would such a church not be in danger of surfeiting itself with rich devotional fare? As Trevor Lloyd rightly warns: 'A church proclaiming a Calvary outside a city wall should beware of putting on more and more services inside the church walls attended only by the very committed.'[67] Jesus did not die for the church — he died for the world. It is the world — and not just the church — which needs to hear the message. Evangelism, and not just devotion, should be on the church's agenda for Holy Week.

The evangelistic potential of Holy Week is helpfully presented by Colin Marchant in material prepared for a *Baptist Union Evangelism Year Book 1968/1969*. Although somewhat dated, if a church could capture the spirit of what is suggested, it would still make quite an impact on the neighbourhood. As Colin Marchant so rightly says: 'We have been too introspective. The Church has kept Holy

Week to itself; choral pieces, communion services, meditations. . . . But Easter is Gospel. It needs telling — in every way possible'.[68]

- *Palm Sunday* (Mark 11:1–11) 'Christ leads his disciples into the city'.
  Call all members together for this day. In the morning prepare children. . . . Help in distribution of leaflets, etc. In the afternoon provide church tea. . . . Go through programme, etc. Evening Service — commission church. Send out letters, etc.
- *Monday* (Mark 11:2–26) 'Into Action'.
  Presentation in music or drama. . . . In evening, modern drama and/or music. Inviations to be definite. . . . Admission by 'contact' only!
- *Tuesday* (Mark 11:27–12:40) 'Controversy'.
  Public debate or forum. Get local celebrities, humanists and a good Christian debater! Invite sixth forms, local debating societies, press.
- *Wednesday* (Mark 14:1–11) 'The Lord in the home'.
  Open as many homes as possible for house groups. Train leaders, instruct hosts. Ask neighbours, friends, family.
- *Thursday* (Mark 14:43-72) 'Communion — and out!'.
  Gather Christians for communion service — then send them out visiting with invitations for Good Friday and Easter Day. During day let minister arrange home communions for shut-ins and let them become centres for prayer.
- *Good Friday* (Mark 15:1–41) 'Remember the Cross'.
  Procession of witness. Placards at football matches, outside factories (where open), on main roads.
- *Saturday* (Mark 15:42–47) 'The world waits'.
  Open-air work at shops and markets. Leaflet distribution, etc.
- *Easter Day* (Mark 16:1–8) 'He is risen'.
  Festival service in morning. Children participating. Families

invited. 'Emmaus teas' ... asking in lonely, friends, family for this Sunday tea. ... reading Emmaus account, going on to church. Evening baptismal service.
- *Easter Monday* (Mark 16:9–20) 'They went out'.
  Rambles culminating in youth rallies.

Another use of the week leading up to Easter is to hold a children's holiday club in this period, instead of in the more customary last week of the summer holidays.

Evangelism and the Sundays leading up to Easter

Although in this book we are primarily concerned with worship, the evangelistic dimension to worship should certainly not be forgotten, not least at this significant time of the year. One possibility is to use the Sundays leading up to Easter for evangelistic purposes. The mornings and/or evenings of Passion Sunday, Palm Sunday and Easter Sunday could take the form of evangelistic guest services in which the Gospel of the crucified and risen Christ is proclaimed.

14

Celebrating Easter and Ascension
— the Lord is risen!

Easter Sunday

Easter Sunday, the highpoint of the Christian year, is a day for celebration. There are a variety of ways in which we can celebrate the day.

Early morning communion and breakfast

There is no better way to begin Easter Day than with an early morning communion service, and in this way to remember afresh that the crucified saviour of Calvary is the risen Lord of Easter Day. A forty-five minute service should be long enough to incorporate both 'word' and 'sacrament'.

The Easter morning communion may gain a further character of its own by including an opportunity for members of the congregation to renew their baptismal promises. In some more liturgical circles, baptismal vows are traditionally renewed during the Easter Vigil held on the Saturday night of Holy Week. However, as we have already argued, there is a danger of piling up services during Holy Week. Easter Sunday seems a far more natural and appropriate day for such a service — and almost certainly offers larger congregation too!

On such an occasion, encourage parents to bring their children and then stay on for a church breakfast. If necessary the smaller children can be looked after in a creche, but the older ones can sit with their parents and experience the joy of an Easter communion. The early start to the day will no doubt impress itself on the children — and in this way Easter will be something special for them. The special nature of the day would be further reinforced by an appetising church breakfast. To be 'appetising', the breakfast doesn't have to be elaborate, but it does have to be less than stark: coffee and croissants could be quite sufficient, with a variety of cereals available for the children. If church breakfasts are something to be looked forward to, then fellowship is enhanced and a good model is offered to the children.

Open-air sunrise service

For the hardier members of the congregation, this is often popular. Alas, in Britain the weather can be very temperamental. Furthermore, in our part of the world dawn can be a very gradual process: at what stage does one actually celebrate the beginning of Easter Day?

Easter morning praise

Rename the morning service — at least just for this day. Let everybody know that Easter Day is a special day.

One welcome custom, borrowed from the Orthodox churches, is to begin the Easter services with the Easter greeting:

> The Lord is risen!
> He is risen indeed!
> Hallelujah!

For maximum effect, it may be necessary for the worship leader to get the congregation to repeat the greeting several times, encouraging people to give full expression to these words of triumph. The Easter greeting is not to be said in the same tones as the words of the 'grace' — it is a festal shout!

If the children normally go out to their Sunday School lessons after the first fifteen to twenty minutes of family worship, there is something to be said for extending their time with the rest of the church family, and in this way impressing on their minds the special nature of the day. Let them be involved in more than the briefest act of praise — for they too need to sense the note of joy and jubilation. What is more, ensure that they actually hear the Easter Gospel read — maybe in dramatic form. How easy it is to deprive children of the actual good news, and instead talk to them about caterpillars and butterflies!

Easter evening celebration

Again, the special nature of the day needs to be emphasised. One simple way is to begin the service a little later than normal, perhap at 7 pm instead of 6.30 pm. Ideally this service — and the morning service too — should have an evangelistic flavour. Outsiders are more likely to attend church on this Sunday than at any other time apart from Christmas. According to a survey, 15% of adults (14+) in the U.K. are to be found in church on an average Sunday (ie, 6.5 million). However, on Easter Sunday this figure is doubled. No doubt many more would go to church on this day if they were given a special invitation.

Traditionally Easter Sunday is a day for baptism. If there are no candidates, then it is good at least to ensure that testimonies ('I have seen the Lord') are given within a service structured with the needs of visitors and guests in mind. This is a day for proclamation as well as celebration.

Easter carol service

Another idea for celebrating the resurrection of Jesus is to hold an Easter carol service in which Easter hymns, both old and new, are combined with Easter readings. One possibility, for instance, would be to divide the final chapters of John's Gospel into seven separate readings. For example:

1) John 19:38–42 The burial of Jesus
2) John 20:1–9   Peter and John at the tomb

3) John 20:10–18   The risen Lord appears to Mary
4) John 20:19–23   The risen Lord appears to the ten disciples
5) John 20:24–29   The risen Lord appears to Thomas
6) John 21:1–14   The risen Lord appears by the lakeside
7) John 21:15–25   The risen Lord appears to Peter

Easter preaching

Easter is a glorious occasion for preaching the good news of Christ crucified and risen. It is a day for apologetic preaching — encouraging the congregation to examine the evidence and to face the facts. It is a day for pastoral preaching — drawing out the implications of Christ's resurrection for our own mortality. It is also an occasion for kerygmatic preaching — the risen Lord Jesus is, by virtue of his death and resurrection, Lord not just of the church but also the world.

One thing is for sure: Easter Day must never be an occasion for sentimental preaching. Charles Hutchins draws attention to how in villages Easter can be much nearer a folk celebration of new life in nature with nearby fields displaying lambs, the hedgerows, snowdrops, primroses and daffodils: 'But Easter must also be proclaimed as *contrary* to "nature" — a point well taken in the Southern hemisphere, where it falls during the Autumn'.[69]

Finally, note that Easter preaching must never be confined to Easter Day. The theme is too large. Michael Perham and Kenneth Stevenson urge 'a rediscovery of the integrity and development of the Easter season', drawing attention to the fact that Eastertide covers 'that great fifty days of celebration that lasts uninterrupted until Evening Prayer on Pentecost Sunday'.[70] Certainly, there is no reason why a series of Easter sermons cannot be preached on the six Sundays following Easter Day. However, the Easter message cannot be limited to Eastertide either. Strictly speaking, every Sunday is a celebration of the fact that Christ rose from the dead on the first day of the week. Every Sunday calls for a proclamation of the risen Lord.

Ascension Day

For probably two reasons, the 'feast' of the Ascension tends to be neglected by the Free Churches. In the first place, Ascension Day always falls mid-week: the fortieth day after Easter Day inevitably happens to be a Thursday, and so does not gain the high profile which other special days of the Christian year tend to have when linked to a particular Sunday. Secondly, and perhaps more importantly, in the modern mind there appears to be some embarrassment about celebrating a festival which seems to be linked to a three-decker view of the universe.

If Ascension Day is, therefore, to be rescued and meaningfully celebrated, two things probably need to be done. First of all, such a celebration is most easily centralised within the worship life of a church by marking the day either the Sunday before or the Sunday after. Mid-week services, for better or for worse, tend to be the province of the committed church core. Secondly, celebration needs to take place within a context of understanding. The meaning of the event needs to be unpacked: not only is the Ascension the end of one chapter in the life of Jesus ('mission accomplished!'), it also marks the beginning of a new chapter ('Jesus is Lord!'), and anticipates the final chapter ('He shall come again!'). All these themes lend themselves for celebration — in traditional hymn and in modern song.

15

Celebrating Pentecost and Trinity
— one God in three persons

Whitsunday

Whitsunday — in some circles more commonly known as
Pentecost — is, along with Christmas and Easter, the third
main Christian festival. As I once wrote in *Family*, it is 'the
Christian equivalent of 5th November. . . . On that day God
set fire to his church! The Holy Spirit came down in power
and, whoosh, the church rocketed into orbit! In more ways
than one that first Christian Pentecost was quite a spectacle.'

But how do we celebrate Whitsunday? 'With difficulty'
was the answer before the advent of charismatic renewal.
Many of the hymns in the section of the hymnbook devoted
to the Holy Spirit were veritable dirges. Fortunately today
we have access to a far greater variety of worship material.

Some people may have difficulty in celebrating Whitsunday
in so far as the Holy Spirit is not called to be the object of our
worship. He is the one who enlivens our worship as we seek
to worship the Father through the Son. And yet surely we
have reason to thank God for the gift of his Spirit, recognising
not simply his initial outpouring some 2,000 years ago, but
his constant coming to his people day by day. In some senses
Whitsunday is the most contemporary of festivals.

It seems to me that Whitsunday is a festival on which
churches should major. This is not a Sunday for the pastor to
be away. Just as no pastor worth their salt would dream of
missing celebrating Christmas or Easter with their people, so

too should no pastor dream of missing Whitsun. For a pastor to go away at Whitsun is surely tantamount to saying to people that the gift of the Spirit is quite unimportant — clearly not the most helpful or true of messages!

Whitsunday is, indeed, a major Christian festival. True, it may no longer feature in the world's calendar, but it most certainly must feature in the church's calendar. The children of the church, for instance, must sense the importance of the occasion. As was suggested for Easter Day, on this Sunday they should not be sent out to their Sunday School lessons with the rapidity that is the norm. Lengthen the opening act of worship. After the opening hymn and prayer, read the story of the first Christian Pentecost; follow it with another song, then follow the song with a brief children's spot in which the message of Whitsun is clarified in terms that they can understand, and follow this with further songs celebrating the gift of the Spirit. Only then may they be free to go out to their own classes. In such a way let them know that Whitsunday is a special day.

Whitsunday provides an ideal opportunity for pastors to give teaching on the Holy Spirit. And such teaching is still sorely needed. There continues to be much confusion concerning the person and work of the Holy Spirit. To fail to grasp this particular nettle — and in some churches it is indeed a nettle — is asking for trouble. Churches need a lead. If pastors are fearful in giving a lead — and some are — then their people will look for a lead elsewhere. Unfortunately this lead elsewhere often results in excess and division within fellowships which, until that moment, were relatively united.

This means that pastors must face up to the challenge presented by 1 Corinthians 12–14. On the other hand, the challenge of other passages which centre on the Holy Spirit and his work must not be neglected either (for example, the great 'Paraclete' sayings of our Lord in John 14–16). A balance must be achieved, for instance, between the fruit and the gifts of the Spirit, if God's people are to be rounded people.

Whitsunday is a day for renewal, both individual and corporate. 'Come Holy Spirit' is our prayer as we celebrate God's gracious outpouring of his Spirit. Whitsunday — if not the whole weekend — can be the occasion for a church to hold an inner mission, a spiritual 10,000 mile service as it were. Whitsun is an occasion for reflection and rededication.

However, Whitsunday is also a day for mission. No church can afford to be completely inward looking on this occasion. Jesus himself linked the themes of the Spirit and mission together when he told his disciples: 'You will receive power when the Holy Spirit comes upon you and you shall be my witnesses' (Acts 1:8). Whitsunday is therefore a day for witness — a day when God's people declare their experience of God's activity in their lives. Such witness may take various forms. It may involve individuals giving their 'testimonies' within the context of a festival service. Better still, it may involve individuals 'making a good confession' within the waters of baptism — indeed, it was on the first Christian Pentecost that 3,000 responded to the Good News of the Gospel and were baptised. But the church's witness must not be confined within the walls of church buildings. Whitsunday is surely also a day for going out and witnessing in the neighbourhood to the power of Jesus to save. Such witness may take the form of a short open-air service in a local park; alternatively it may involve cancelling the evening service and the whole congregation going from door to door, seeking opportunities to share the Good News with others.

Mission, of course, goes far beyond the locality. The Lord Jesus, for instance, linked the gift of the Spirit with witness to the 'ends of the earth' (Acts 1:8). Indeed, it was on the first Whitsunday that Parthians, Medes, Elamites and many others for the first time heard 'the wonders of God' declared in their own tongues (Acts 2:8–11). With this in mind, another way of celebrating Whitsunday would be to make it one of the church's missionary Sundays, when the work of its (link-) missionaries is highlighted. Here again there can be all kinds of creative ways to impart information and inspiration. In the old days churches were dependent on missionary deputations. In these days of modern technology, it is often possible to contact missionaries direct by phone during the service!

Trinity Sunday

Trinity Sunday, the Sunday after Whitsunday, is the most difficult of Christian festivals to celebrate. As the worship manual *Praise God* (p 41) rightly says: 'The other seasons of the Christian year celebrate historical events. "Trinity" is the celebration of a way of expressing truth.' No Christian doctrine is more difficult to express — indeed, the history of the church bears painful witness to the difficulties experienced by many a theologian. Nonetheless, it does the preacher and congregation good occasionally to wrestle with the church's affirmation as stated in the Athanasian Creed: 'We worship one God in Trinity and Trinity in Unity; neither confounding the Persons, nor dividing the Substance.' The preacher should be able to show that ultimately we are not dealing with metaphysical speculation, but rather with a theological formulation which brings to explicit expression truths which are implicit and fundamental to the Christian faith.

At the end of the day, it must be confessed that the doctrine of the Trinity surpasses thought. However, where thought fails, worship can continue. One of the joys of preparing for Trinity Sunday is to discover the sheer variety of worship material that can be used. Sermons may be limited — but worship never!

16

Celebrating the Church Anniversary

— Happy Birthday everyone!

Church anniversaries are not necessarily summer occasions. However, if my diary is anything to go by, the month of May is the most popular time in the year for such a celebration. Whatever the time, ensure that the children of the church sense something of the joyful nature of the occasion. There should be a large birthday cake (with candles?) on the Communion Table to emphasise that a church anniversary is indeed the church's birthday. Why not hang balloons around the church, as if it were a party. The celebrations could then continue after the service, when coffee and cake could be served.

The question arises: what are we trying to achieve through celebrating a church anniversary? What is the raison d'être of this particular festival?

To my mind there are three basic thrusts to a church anniversary:

A backward look

In the first place, a church anniversary is a time for looking back and thanking God for his faithfulness. Unless it is a particularly young church, one can normally look back over a good number of years of Christian witness. Many free churches, for instance, can trace their origins back one hundred years or more, while others can look back over two or three centuries. Such churches can thank God for the way in which their spiritual forefathers endured persecution and imprisonment for the sake of the faith. It's good to be reminded of such history. Sometimes we jump all too quickly over the centuries in our hurry to get back to the pages of the New Testament. On many a church anniversary Sunday, I like to choose a hymn which goes back to our roots — it may be an early Anabaptist composition or one of the great hymns of the Protestant Reformation. Such hymns call to mind the words of the Psalmist: 'One generation will commend your works to another; they will tell of your might acts' (Ps 145:4). Psalm 145 is indeed a splendid church anniversary psalm — with its vivid reminder that we are not the first to believe in Christ.

Yes, it's good to be able to look back and be mindful of the church's history a generation or more ago. However, in looking back it is important not to forget the immediate past. Every church celebrating its anniversary should be conscious of what God has done among them even over the past twelve months. Needless to say, it is at this point that the visiting preacher has no contribution to make — he or she has no idea of how God has blessed the fellowship. It needs the resident pastor — or even better one of the 'ordinary' members — to articulate the way in which God has blessed his people over the past year.

As one who is frequently asked to conduct church anniversaries, my own particular custom as a visiting preacher is to ask for a church testimony in the morning service. I stress that what I have in mind is not the kind of report that the church secretary might give at the annual church meeting, but rather a four-minute contribution in which one of the members of the church highlights three or four aspects of the church's recent life. This then stimulates prayer: for having heard of God's goodness, the congregation will naturally want to express its praise and thanksgiving to God — whether or not that prayer is led by the visiting preacher or by another member of the congregation is immaterial.

As for the evening service of a church anniversary, why not ask for a personal testimony of someone who has been blessed in their own personal life over the past twelve months? God blesses in so many ways. It may well be that the testimony is given by one who has been converted and baptised in the past twelve months. On the other hand, it could equally be that the testimony is given by someone who has been bereaved over the past twelve months and in that bereavement has known something of the sustaining love of God. Ideally, the testimony should lead individual members of the congregation to reflect on how God has blessed them in the past year, and this in turn will evoke further praise.

A forward look

Yes, church anniversaries are an occasion for looking backwards with thanksgiving. But they are also opportunities for looking forwards with anticipation to the year that lies ahead. It is at this point that there is a very real role for the visiting preacher. For the Holy Spirit can use him or her as a catalyst to give a broader vision of God's purposes to the local fellowship. However, if the guest preacher's sermons are to be truly inspiring, then it would be helpful if the preacher could have some idea of where the church is spiritually. In this respect it is helpful if pastors and/or church secretaries send on to the visiting preacher recent church magazines or newsletters, for they will probably indicate some of the issues which are on the church's agenda. At the end of the day the visiting preacher may still be shooting in the dark, but at least the preacher will know in which direction he or she should be facing. Whatever, let the visiting preacher encourage the congregation to take hold of William Carey's great maxim 'Expect great things from God. Attempt great things for God'.

However great the church's past may have been, point the congregation to the future: for we are not called to be sunset people dreaming of the past, but sunrise people dreaming of the future. A church anniversary is an occasion for vision and for faith. For our God 'is able to do immeasurably more than all we ask or imagine, according to his power that is at work within us' (Eph 3:20).

Focusing on the present

Finally, there is a third dimension to church anniversaries: in addition to the backward and forward look, there is also the present aspect. The church anniversary provides a splendid opportunity to pray for those for whom public prayer is rarely made in the church — the pastor and his or her partner. If there is a communion service — and if ever a day is appropriate for such a service, it is then — why not get the pastor and his or her partner to kneel at the Communion Table while the church focuses their prayers on them. It can be a moving experience for everybody.

Prayer will, of course, not be limited to the couple in the manse. A church anniversary Sunday is, for instance, a good occasion to pray for all those who have come to church over the past twelve months for a special service of some kin or other: parents who have brought their children for a service of dedication; young people — and indeed not so young people — who have confessed their faith in the water of baptism; couples who have pledged their love for one another; those who have come to mark the death of a loved one ... all these can be the object of prayer at church anniversary time.

17

Celebrating Harvest
— a festival with a difference

From one perspective, harvest marks the end of the year. From a church perspective, it often marks the beginning of the year — for it is towards the end of September that many churches move into a higher gear after the summer holidays.

In some quarters it has become fashionable to dismiss harvest services. Some people object that harvest is not a specifically Christian festival, but has its origins in some pagan festival. Certainly, unlike the other major Christian festivals, it is not rooted in the life of Jesus. But does a festival have to be specifically Christocentric to be Christian? Do we Christians not have a doctrine of creation as well as a doctrine of redemption?

I believe there is a lot to be said for celebrating harvest. It can be argued that there are three occasions in the year when many people feel sentimental and are inclined to go to church: Christmas, Easter and Harvest. If this is so, then surely for the Gospel's sake we should take advantage of sentimentality and not be ashamed to celebrate harvest.

But, it might be further objected, does it really make sense to celebrate harvest in the inner city, where people, if they've seen a plough at all, have only seen some relic in a museum? Can what is essentially a rural festival be transferred to the town? Can a city congregation with integrity sing 'We plough the fields and scatter the good seed on the ground'? I fail to see why not. Even though most people today do not

175

know the great sense of relief at getting the harvest safely in, we should surely be grateful for our packet soups and our tins of baked beans! We may not have had a direct hand in their production, and yet we can and should express gratitude to God for his provision.

So let's cash in on sentimentality and celebrate harvest — provided our celebrations are not in themselves sentimental. Some token display will still be needed to foster sentiment and encourage the irregulars to attend church that Sunday. But on the whole, do not major on gifts of kind, but rather on gifts of cash. Harvest today is a time to remember the needs of the less fortunate. While thanking God for his material goodness, we need to speak about people's meanness towards one another. We need to arouse people's consciences to the needs of the Third World.

Harvest is, in fact, an occasion to be forthright. It is an occasion for pulling at the heartstrings — and for most of us those heartstrings are in need of exercise! We have hardened our hearts to the needs of the poor. 'Weep with those who weep' declare the Scriptures (Rom 12:15), but when did we last shed a tear for the miserable poor? Tears, of course, like prayers are not enough — they will never fill an empty belly. Hard cash is needed.

With the help of an overhead projector one can work out the contents of the average shopping basket that week. Indeed, one can take one's own bill from the supermarket, multiply it by the number of families in the church, and then say that is how much the church needs to raise that Harvest Sunday for söme project in the Third World. The perspective gained can be frighteningly challenging. Harvest is an occasion for prophetic preaching in the style of the great eighth century (BC) prophets: 'Let justice roll on like a river, righteousness like a never-failing stream' (Amos 5:24).

Harvest is also an occasion for evangelistic preaching. The parables form a happy hunting ground for sermon material. For example, the rich fool who desired to build bigger barns

(Lk 12:16–21); the wheat and the weeds destined for ulti-
mate separation (Mt 13:24–30), and Lazarus and the rich
man (Lk 16:19–31). Alternatively, some of the great texts in
John's Gospel lend themselves to the occasion: 'If anyone is
thirsty, let him come to me and drink' (Jn 8:37), words
spoken at a Jewish harvest festival; or 'I am the bread of life.
He who comes to me will never go hungry' (Jn 6:35). This is
a day to seek a harvest of souls!

Clearly, the way in which the worship is ordered at a
harvest festival will vary according to the purpose in mind.
Some of the great traditional harvest hymns will need to be
sung. No harvest is complete without 'Come you thankful
people come' or 'We plough the fields and scatter'. The
Psalms provide a wonderful resource for stimulating praise:
for example, Psalms 65 and 67. Prayers will surely be offered
for the many people in the third world who are in need —
and for the agencies which seek to meet those needs.
Harvest services need to cover a wide gamut of human
emotion: along with thanksgiving there needs to be repentance, along with prayers of intercession for the needy there
must also be a recognition of our own need of God. Such
services pose a great challenge to the worship leader — but
where the challenge is met, great satisfaction is surely
derived.

Conclusion

Worship is the raison d'être of the church. In the final analysis, the church doesn't exist to tell others the good news of Jesus Christ; nor does it exist to help the world to be a better place. The church exists for God. In the words of the Westminster Shorter Catechism, 'Man's chief end is to glorify God and to enjoy him for ever.' What is true of man is even more true of the church. We are 'a people for his praise' (Isaiah 43:21; also 1 Peter 2:5, 9).

To lead a congregation in worship is to be entrusted with one of the most important tasks in the life of the church. It is my hope that this book will have enabled the reader to discharge that responsibility all the more effectively. This book does not pretend to be a complete guide to all that takes place in worship. Nor does it pretend to be *the* guide, in the sense of seeking to lay down definitive rules and regulations for the conduct of worship. It does, however, set out to deal with some of the general principles that lie behind the art and science of leading God's people in worship, and then apply those principles to the Christian festivals many a church will celebrate in any given year. At the end of the day, however, it is God alone who gives life to our worship. In the words of Ernest Payne and Stephen Winward, 'To have the right pattern and forms is not enough. They may be "faultily faultless, icily regular, splendidly null". The use of forms without the Holy Spirit becomes formalism, as deadly as an enemy to true worship as formlessness'.[71]

The prayer behind this book is that the Holy Spirit will so touch the worship of God's people that the pedestrian and unimaginative might be transformed into joyful celebrations of the faith. Celebrations which will enable worshippers meaningfully to express their worship and their love, their confession and their commitment, their concern and their prayer, and provide a fitting context in which the word might be proclaimed.

Bibliography

Abba, Raymond, *Principles of Christian Worship with special reference to the Free Churches* (OUP: London, 1957).

Administry, *Let us pray. Planning times of corporate prayer* (Administry, 28 Fontmell Close, St Albans, Herts, AL3 5HU).

von Allman, J. J., *Worship, Its Theology and Practice* [English translation] (Lutterworth: London, 1965).

Baptist Union of Scotland, *A Manual for Worship* (Glasgow)

Beasley-Murray, Paul, *Why be baptized and become a church member?* Baptist Basics No 6, (Baptist Union: London).
What do we do at the Lord's Supper? Baptist Basics No 7 (Baptist Union: London).

Blackwood, Andrew, *The Fine Art of Christian Worship* (Abingdon: Nashville, TN, 1939).

Buchanan, Colin, *Patterns of Sunday Worship,* Grove Booklet on Ministry Worship No 9 (Grove: Bramcote, Notts, 1972).
Encountering Charismatic Worship, Grove Booklet on Ministry Worship No 51 (Grove: Bramcote, Notts, 1977).
Liturgy for Initiation, Grove Booklet on Ministry and Worship No 65 (Grove Bramcote, Notts, 1979).
Leading Worship, Grove Worship Series No 76 (Grove: Bramcote, Notts, 1981).
The Kiss of Peace, Grove Worship Series No 80, (Grove: Bramcote, Notts, 1982).

Carson, Herbert, *Hallelujah! Christian Worship* (Evangelical Press: Welwyn, Herts, 1980).

Clark, Neville, *Call To Worship* (SCM: London, 1960).

Cutts, David, *Worship in Small Congregations,* Grove Worship Series No 108 (Grove: Bramcote, Notts, 1988).

Dunstan, Alan, *Interpreting Worship* (Mowbrays: London, 1984).

Earnshaw, Leslie, *Worship for the Seventies* (Denholm House Press: Nutfield, Surrey, 1973).

Fellingham, David, *Worship Restored* (Kingsway: Eastbourne, 1987).

Forrester, Duncan, McDonald, J. I. H., and Tellini, Gian, *Encounter with God* (T and T Clark: Edinburgh, 1983).

Foster, Richard, *Celebration of Discipline* (Hodder and Stoughton: London, 1984).

Gilmore, Alec, Smalley, Edward, and Walker, Michael, *Praise God — a collection of resource material for Christian worship* (Baptist Union: London, 1980).

Green, Bernard, *The Blessing of Infants and the Dedication of Parents,* Baptist Basics No 1 (Baptist Union: London).

Gunstone, John, *A People for His Praise. Renewal & Congregational Life* (Hodder and Stoughton: London, 1978).

Jasper, Ronald C. D., Ed., *The Renewal of Worship. Essays by members of the Joint Liturgical Group* (OUP: London, 1965).

Kennedy, David, and Mann, David, *Sunday Evening Worship,* Grove Worship Series No 109 (Grove: Bramcote, Notts, 1989).

Kendrick, Graham, Ed., *Worship* (Kingsway: Eastbourne, 1984). *Ten Worshipping Churches* (MARC: London, 1987).

Kreider, Eleanor, *Enter His Gates. Fitting Worship Together* (Marshall Pickering: London, 1989).

Leach, John, *Liturgy and Liberty* (MARC: Eastbourne, 1989).

Lloyd, Trevor, *Informal Liturgy — an examination of the possibilities of non-sacramental worship* Grove Booklet on Ministry and Worship No 6, (Grove: Bramcote, Notts, 1972). *Introducing Liturgical Change,* Grove Worship Series No 87 (Grove: Bramcote, Notts, 1987).

Martin, Ralph P., *Worship in the Early Church* (Marshall, Morgan and Scott: London, 1964). *The Worship of God — some theological, pastoral and practical reflections* (Paternoster: Exeter, 1982).

Maxwell, William D., *An Outline of Worship. Its Developments and Forms* [revised]. (OUP: London, 1945). *Concerning Worship* (OUP: London, 1948).

Morrow, Thomas M., *Worship and Preaching* (Epworth: London, 1956).

Moule, C. F. D., *Worship in the New Testament* (Lutterworth: London, 1961).

Ortlund, Anne, *Up With Worship* (Regal: Glendale, California, 1975)

Owen, David, *Sharers in Worship* (National Christian Education Council: Redhill, Surrey, 1980).

Payne, Ernest A., and Winward, Stephen, *Orders and Prayers for Christian Worship* (Baptist Union: London, 1960).

Perham, Michael, *Liturgy, Pastoral and Parochial* (SPCK: London, 1984).

Perham, Michael and Stevenson, Kenneth, *Waiting for the Risen Christ. Commentary on 'Lent, Holy Week, Easter: Services & Prayers'* (SPCK: London, 1986).

Prime, Derek, *Created to Praise* (Hodder and Stoughton: London, 1981).

Spurgeon, Charles H., *Lectures To My Students I* (Passmore and Alabaster: London, 1897).

Taylor, Michael, *Variations on a Theme — some guidelines for everyday Christians who want to reform the liturgy* (Galliard: London, 1973).

Tennant, David F., *Children In the Church. A Baptist View* (Baptist Publications: London, 1978).

Vasey, Michael, *Intercessions in Worship,* Grove Worship Series No 77 (Grove: Bramcote, Notts, 1981).

Wainwright, Geoffrey, *Doxology. A Systematic Theology* (Epworth: London, 1980).

Walker, Michael, *The Lord's Supper* (Baptist Union: London, 1981).

Infant Dedication (Baptist Union: London, 1987).

Wallace, Jamie, *What Happens in Worship?* (Baptist Union: London, 1982).

White, James F., *Introduction to Christian Worship* (Abingdon: Nashville, TN 1980).

White, R. E. O., *A Guide to Pastoral Care* (Pickering and Inglis: London, 1976).

Wilkinson, John, *Family and Evangelistic Services* (Church Information Office: London, 1967).

Williams, Dick, Ed., *Prayers for Today's Church* (CPAS: London, 1972).

Winward, Stephen, *Responsive Praises and Prayers for Minister and Congregation* (Hodder and Stoughton: London, 1958).

The Reformation of our Worship (Carey Kingsgate Press: London, 1964).

Celebration and Order — a guide to worship and the lectionary (Baptist Union: London, 1981).

Yorkshire Baptist Association, *Christian Worship — some contemporary issues* (Leeds, 1984).

Notes

1. J. J. von Allmen, *Worship: Its Theology and Practice* (Lutterworth: London, 1965), p 15.
2. Anne Ortlund, *Is Your Church Real?* (Regal, California), pp 3–4.
3. Alan Dunstan, *Interpreting Worship* (Mowbrays: London, 1984), p 7.
4. Ralph Martin, *The Worship of God* (Paternoster: Exeter, 1982), p 5.
5. *Ibid.*, pp 23–24.
6. F. H. Brabant, quoted in Raymond Abba, *Principles of Christian Worship With Special Reference to the Free Churches* (OUP: London, 1957).
7. Jamie Wallace, *What Happens in Worship?* (Baptist Union: London, 1982), p 5.
8. George Beasley-Murray, *Matthew* (Scripture Union: London, 1984), p 33.
9. Eleanor Kreider, *Enter His Gates* (Marshall Pickering: London, 1989), p 76.
10. J. J. von Allmen, *op. cit.*, p 171.
11. Eleanor Kreider, *op. cit.*, pp 62–63.
12. John Leach, *Liturgy and Liberty* (MARC: Eastbourne, 1989), p 18.
13. Charles H. Spurgeon, *Lectures to My Students I* (Passmore and Alabaster: London, 1897), p 56.
14. Geoffrey Wainwright, *Doxology: A Systematic Theology* (Epworth: London, 1980), p 38.
15. Thomas M. Morrow, *Worship and Preaching* (Epworth: London, 1956), p 13.

16. Geoffrey Wainwright, *op. cit.*, p 40.
17. R. E. O. White, *A Guide to Pastoral Care* (Pickering and Inglis: London, 1976), p 29.
18. Stephen Winward, *Celebration and Order* (Baptist Union: London, 1981), p 28.
19. Isaac Watts, quoted in Stephen Winward, *Responsive Prayers and Praises for Minister and Congregation* (Hodder and Stoughton: London, 1958), p 3.
20. C. F. D. Moule, *Worship in the New Testament* (Lutterworth: London, 1961), p 73.
21. Stephen Winward, *Celebration and Order*, p 29.
22. Charles H. Spurgeon, *op. cit.*, p 55.
23. Dick France, *Matthew* (IVP: Leicester, 1986), p 128.
24. R. E. O. White, *op. cit.*, p 29.
25. Michael Vasey, *Intercessions in Worship* (Grove: Bramcote, Notts, 1981), p 22.
26. Michael Baughen, *Let Us Pray* (Administry paper on prayer), p 16.
27. Michael Taylor, *Variations on a Theme* (Galliard: London, 1973), p 73.
28. Charles H. Spurgeon, *op. cit.*, p 159.
29. *Ibid.*, p 71.
30. Raymond Abba, *op. cit.*, p 50.
31. R. E. O. White, *op. cit.*, p 28.
32. Charles H. Spurgeon, *op. cit.*, pp 88–89.
33. William Maxwell, *Concerning Worship* (OUP: London, 1958), p 56.
34. Ronald C. D. Jasper, Ed., *The Renewal of Worship* (OUP: London, 1965), p 7.
35. Ernest A. Payne and Stephen Winward, *Orders and Prayers for Christian Worship* (Baptist Union: London, 1960), p xii.
36. C. F. D. Moule, *op. cit.*, pp 62–63.
37. J. J. von Allmen, *op. cit.*, p 156.
38. *Ibid.*, p 130.
39. Ernest A. Payne and Stephen Winward, *op. cit.*, pp 179–181.
40. Michael Walter, *The Lord's Supper* (Baptist Union: London, 1981), p 12.
41. C. F. D. Moule, *op. cit.*, pp 42–43.

42. Graham Kendrick, Ed., *Ten Worshipping Churches* (MARC: London, 1987), p 16.
43. Ralph Martin, *op. cit.*, p 13.
44. John Leach, *op. cit.*, p 17.
45. Trevor Lloyd, *Introducing Liturgical Change* (Grove: Bramcote, Notts), p 17.
46. Andrew Blackwood, *The Fine Art of Christian Worship* (Abingdon: Nashville, TN, 1939), p 153.
47. J. J. von Allmen, *op. cit.*, p 142.
48. C. F. D. Moule, *op. cit.*, pp 78–79.
49. Tom Smail, Editorial in *Renewal* magazine (Autumn, 1976).
50. John Gunstone, *A People for His Praise* (Hodder and Stoughton: London, 1978), p 39.
51. Colin Buchanan, *Leading Worship* (Grove: Bramcote, Notts, 1981), p 21.
52. Stephen Winward, *op. cit.*, p 23.
53. Alec Gilmore, Edward Smalley and Michael Walker, *Praise God* (Baptist Union: London, 1980), p 139.
54. *Ibid.*, p 139.
55. Colin Buchanan, *Revising the ASB* (Grove: Bramcote, Notts, 1989), p 21.
56. Alec Gilmore, Edward Smalley and Michael Walker, *op. cit.*, p 140.
57. *Ibid.*, p 140.
58. David Watson, *I Believe in Evangelism* (Hodder and Stoughton: London, 1979), p 166.
59. *Ibid.*, pp 156–157.
60. Michael Perham, *Liturgy Pastoral and Parochial* (SPCK: London, 1984), p 152.
61. David Tripp, *A New Dictionary of Liturgy and Worship* (SCM, London, 1986), p 540ff.
62. Trevor Lloyd, *Celebrating Lent, Holy Week and Easter* (Grove: Bramcote, Notts, 1985), p 10.
63. *Ibid.*, p 73.
64. Marian E. Musselthwaite, *The Church Family at Worship* (NCEC, Nutfield, Surrey, 1968), p 63.
65. Michael Perham, *op. cit.*, p 172ff.
66. Philip Gouldson, Eds., Derek Wensley and Brian Frost, *Celebration* (Galliard: London, 1970), pp 24–28.

67. Trevor Lloyd, *op. cit.*, p 10.
68. Colin Marchant, *Baptist Union Evangelism Year Book 1968/1969*.
69. Charles Hutchins, *Preaching on Special Occasions* (Grove: Bramcote, Notts, 1984), p 8ff.
70. Michael Perham and Kenneth Stevenson, *Waiting for the Risen Christ* (SPCK: London, 1986).
71. Ernest A. Payne and Stephen Winward, *op. cit.*, p xiii.

Dynamic Leadership

by Paul Beasley-Murray

Without a vision the people perish.

A church with vision is one that grows. To gain a vision a church needs effective leadership. This book, by one of Britian's most eminent Christians, shows us clearly and biblically how to develop dynamic leaders.

Using many models from the wider world, but, above all, the model of Jesus himself, Paul Beasley-Murray shows us how to lead, and, just as important, who can lead. For truly dynamic leadership is shared in a team, where tasks can be defined, goals accomplished, and the whole church served in a Christ-like way.

This book is profoundly practical. How do you inspire the youth group? Lead a church meeting? Motivate the church for evangelism? Train new believers? Instil Christian values in your community? Here again dynamic leadership is the name of the game.

Reading this book could change your church for ever.

'Excellent...full of practical insights for busy church leaders.'

—**Stephen Gaukroger, author of** *It Makes Sense*

MARC
Monarch Publications

Churches With Roots

by Johan Lukasse

THE CONVERSION OF PAGAN EUROPE

Christianity has been privatised!

For most Europeans the Christian faith has become, at best, a matter of private interest. It has lost its force for social, political or moral change. Europe is the only continent in the world in which the Christian faith is actually declining.

'What Europe needs today,' insists Johan Lukasse, 'is a living, powerful, Christ-centred church; churches through which the risen Lord is at work and which He uses as His instrument to make known His plan of redemption.'

This extremely practical volume offers a host of suggestions for church planting in the UK and Europe: cells for growth and discipleship, dealing with dead churches, evangelism by presence and proclamation, spiritual warfare, degrees of resistance, mistakes to avoid, and much more.

JOHAN LUKASSE is President of the Belgian Evangelical Mission. Concerned by the slow spread of the gospel, he started using teams for church planting in 1972. Since then he and his colleagues have been responsible for establishing a number of new churches, and his knowledge and experience are widely valued.

Co-published with STL Books and the Belgian Evangelical Mission.

MARC
Monarch Publications

Monarch Publications

Monarch Publications was founded to produce books from a
Christian perspective which challenge the way people think
and feel. Our books are intended to appeal to a very wide
constituency, in order to encourage Christian values which
currently seem to be in decline.

Monarch Publications has three imprints:

<u>Monarch</u> is concerned with issues, to develop the mind.

<u>MARC</u> is a skills-based list, concentrating on leadership and
mission.

<u>Minstrel</u> concentrates on creative writing, to stimulate the
imagination.

Monarch Publications is owned by The Servant Trust, a
Christian charity run by representatives of the evangelical
church in Britain, committed to serve God in publishing and
music.

For further information on the Trust, including details of
how you may be able to support its work, please write to:

> The Secretary
> The Servant Trust
> 1 St Anne's Road
> Eastbourne
> East Sussex BN21 3UN
> England